Tanza

Everything You Need to Know

Copyright © 2023 by Noah Gil-Smith.

All rights reserved. No part of this book may be reproduced, distributed, or transmitted in any form or by any means, including photocopying, recording, or other electronic or mechanical methods, without the prior written permission of the publisher, except in the case of brief quotations embodied in critical reviews and certain other noncommercial uses permitted by copyright law. This book was created with the assistance of Artificial Intelligence. The content presented in this book is for entertainment purposes only. It should not be considered as a substitute for professional advice or comprehensive research. Readers are encouraged to independently verify any information and consult relevant experts for specific matters. The author and publisher disclaim any liability or responsibility for any loss, injury, or inconvenience caused or alleged to be caused directly or indirectly by the information presented in this book.

Introduction: Unraveling the Enigma of Tanzania 6

The Geographical Diversity of Tanzania: From Kilimanjaro to Zanzibar 8

A Glimpse into Tanzania's Rich History 10

Early Inhabitants and Pre-colonial Cultures 12

Colonial Era and Struggle for Independence 14

The Birth of Modern Tanzania: From Tanganyika to the United Republic 16

Exploring Tanzania's Political Landscape 18

Tanzanian Wildlife: A Journey through the Savannah and Beyond 20

National Parks and Conservation Efforts 22

Discovering the Unique Flora and Fauna of Tanzania 24

Culinary Traditions of the Tanzanian Table 26

Savoring the Delicacies of Swahili Cuisine 28

Zanzibar: A Spice-infused Paradise 30

Experiencing Wildlife Safaris: The Tanzanian Safari Magic 32

Exploring Serengeti National Park: A Wildlife Spectacle 34

Ngorongoro Crater: Nature's Sunken Paradise 36

The Wonders of Selous Game Reserve 38

Mount Kilimanjaro: Scaling Africa's Tallest Peak 40

The Stunning Beauty of Lake Victoria 42

Zanzibar Archipelago: Tropical Paradise Found 44

Stone Town: A Journey Back in Time 46

Dar es Salaam: Tanzania's Thriving Metropolis 48

Arusha: Gateway to Tanzania's Treasures 50

Mwanza: Port City on the Shores of Lake Victoria 52

Bagamoyo: A Historic Coastal Trading Post 54

Cultural Diversity of Tanzania: A Melting Pot of Traditions 56

The Maasai: Enduring Traditions and Modern Realities 58

The Hadza: Ancient Hunter-Gatherers of Tanzania 60

Makonde: Masters of Wood Carvings 62

Tinga Tinga Art: Vivid Colors and Stories 64

Music and Dance: A Rhythmic Tapestry of Tanzania 66

The Swahili Language: Heartbeat of the Nation 68

Traditional Festivals and Celebrations 70

Spirituality and Religion in Tanzanian Society 72

Education and Literacy: Nurturing Tomorrow's Leaders 74

Healthcare and Challenges in Tanzania 76

The Tanzanian Economy: Past and Present 78

Mining and Natural Resources: Blessing or Curse? 80

Conservation and Environmental Issues 82

Women Empowerment and Gender Equality 84

Sports and Recreation: Passion for Football and Beyond 86

Nurturing the Tanzanian Arts and Literature 88

Infrastructure and Transportation: Connecting the Nation 90

Challenges and Hopes for Tanzania's Future 92

Epilog 94

Introduction: Unraveling the Enigma of Tanzania

Tanzania, a land of captivating mystery and diverse wonders, lies nestled on the eastern coast of Africa, bordered by eight countries, and washed by the vast Indian Ocean to the east. This enchanting nation has long beckoned adventurous souls and intrepid travelers with its awe-inspiring landscapes, teeming wildlife, vibrant cultures, and rich history.

Covering an expansive area of approximately 945,087 square kilometers, Tanzania is home to a remarkable variety of ecosystems, from the sprawling savannahs of the Serengeti and the magnificent Mount Kilimanjaro, the highest peak in Africa, to the pristine beaches and coral reefs of Zanzibar. The country's geographical diversity is a testament to its allure, drawing in nature enthusiasts, thrill-seekers, and curious wanderers alike.

But what sets Tanzania apart from other African nations is not just its breathtaking scenery. It's the captivating history woven into its fabric that adds layers of intrigue to this enigmatic land. With archaeological evidence suggesting human presence dating back two million years, Tanzania's past is as ancient as it is fascinating.

Long before European explorers set foot on its soil, the region was home to various indigenous groups, each with their unique languages, traditions, and customs. Notably, the Maasai, Hadza, and San tribes still maintain their ancestral ways of life, offering a glimpse into the distant past.

European influence on Tanzania began in the 16th century when Portuguese traders sailed along the coast, followed by Arab merchants who established trade routes through the Swahili Coast. In the late 19th century, European colonization intensified, with the German East Africa Company and later the British Empire carving out territories in the region.

The 20th century marked a period of transformation for Tanzania as the struggle for independence gained momentum. Led by visionary leaders like Julius Nyerere, Tanganyika, as it was known then, gained independence in 1961, becoming one of the first African countries to break free from colonial rule. Zanzibar followed suit and later unified with Tanganyika to form the United Republic of Tanzania.

Today, Tanzania is a vibrant nation, celebrating its cultural diversity and preserving its heritage with pride. Swahili, a Bantu language with traces of Arabic influence, is the national language, serving as a unifying thread that binds the country's myriad ethnic groups together.

But it's not just the past that makes Tanzania an enigma; it's also the present and the future that intrigue observers. As a developing nation, Tanzania grapples with a unique set of challenges and opportunities. While strides have been made in education, healthcare, and economic development, there are still hurdles to overcome.

Yet, the people of Tanzania possess an unyielding spirit and an unwavering optimism, which has paved the way for progress and growth. From bustling cities like Dar es Salaam and Arusha to the quiet villages dotted across the countryside, Tanzanians continue to carve their path toward a brighter tomorrow.

In the chapters that follow, we shall embark on an extraordinary journey to explore the essence of Tanzania. From its captivating wildlife and mouthwatering cuisine to its ancient cities and rich cultural traditions, each chapter will reveal a distinct facet of this magnificent country. So, buckle up as we delve deep into the heart of Tanzania, unlocking its secrets and uncovering the true enigma that lies within. Welcome to a land where dreams are woven into reality, and the beauty of Africa flourishes in all its splendor. Welcome to Tanzania!

The Geographical Diversity of Tanzania: From Kilimanjaro to Zanzibar

Tanzania, a country of astounding geographical diversity, is a land that never ceases to amaze with its breathtaking landscapes, ranging from majestic mountains to idyllic tropical islands. Situated in East Africa, Tanzania is bordered by Kenya and Uganda to the north, Rwanda, Burundi, and the Democratic Republic of the Congo to the west, and Zambia, Malawi, and Mozambique to the south. To the east lies the vast expanse of the Indian Ocean, lapping against Tanzania's pristine coastline.

At the heart of Tanzania's geographical allure stands the iconic Mount Kilimanjaro, the highest peak in Africa and the tallest free-standing mountain in the world. Towering at an impressive height of 5,895 meters (19,341 feet) above sea level, Kilimanjaro's snow-capped summit is a sight to behold, drawing climbers and adventurers from across the globe to conquer its formidable slopes.

Beyond Kilimanjaro, Tanzania boasts a diverse range of terrains, encompassing savannahs, grasslands, forests, and mountains. The Serengeti National Park, a UNESCO World Heritage Site, is a vast savannah that hosts the awe-inspiring Great Migration of wildebeest and other herbivores, one of the most remarkable natural phenomena on Earth.

To the southwest, the Ngorongoro Crater, a caldera formed by a massive volcanic eruption, offers a unique ecosystem, teeming with a concentrated population of wildlife, including the Big Five (elephant, lion, leopard, buffalo, and rhino). This geological wonder serves as a natural enclosure, creating a breathtaking amphitheater of wildlife within its walls.

While the inland areas showcase the splendor of the African savannah, the coastline tells a different tale of paradise found. The Zanzibar Archipelago, situated just off the Tanzanian coast, boasts pristine white sandy beaches, crystal-clear turquoise waters, and vibrant coral reefs. Zanzibar Island, the largest among the archipelago, is a cultural melting pot, characterized by its historic Stone Town, a UNESCO World Heritage Site, where ancient Swahili, Arab, Indian, and European influences intertwine.

Moving inland, Tanzania's central regions are adorned with the majestic landscapes of the Southern Highlands, featuring lush green tea plantations, rolling hills, and scenic lakes. The town of Arusha, known as the "Safari Capital of the World," serves as a gateway to many of Tanzania's renowned national parks, making it a bustling hub for wildlife enthusiasts.

Lake Victoria, one of Africa's Great Lakes and the largest tropical lake in the world, also graces Tanzania's northern region. Its waters provide sustenance to countless communities and support an abundance of biodiversity.

In the western reaches of Tanzania lies Gombe Stream National Park, where British primatologist Jane Goodall conducted groundbreaking research on chimpanzees. This protected area showcases the remarkable behavior and intelligence of our closest living relatives, the chimpanzees, allowing visitors to immerse themselves in the world of these fascinating primates.

Beyond the mainland, the Tanzanian waters are home to a diverse marine life, making the country an ideal destination for snorkeling and scuba diving enthusiasts. The Marine Parks and Reserves of Mafia Island and the coasts of Dar es Salaam and Zanzibar offer opportunities to explore vibrant coral reefs, swim with dolphins, and encounter an array of marine species.

A Glimpse into Tanzania's Rich History

As we delve into the annals of time, we encounter a tapestry of fascinating events and cultures that have shaped Tanzania's rich history. The roots of Tanzania's past run deep, stretching back millions of years, leaving traces of early human presence and ancient civilizations that have left their mark on this enigmatic land.

Archaeological discoveries suggest that Tanzania has been inhabited by early hominids for over two million years, making it a region of great significance in our understanding of human evolution. The Olduvai Gorge, located in northern Tanzania, has yielded invaluable fossils and artifacts, offering a glimpse into the lives of our earliest ancestors.

Long before the dawn of written history, various Bantu-speaking tribes inhabited the region, leaving behind a legacy of unique languages, customs, and traditions. Among these diverse groups were the ancestors of the present-day Maasai and Hadza communities, who continue to preserve their distinct ways of life to this day.

The coastal regions of Tanzania saw a vibrant trade network flourish from the 9th century onwards, fueled by the Swahili culture, which was a fusion of African, Arab, and Persian influences. The Swahili city-states, such as Kilwa, Sofala, and Zanzibar, thrived as important centers of trade, connecting East Africa with the Middle East, India, and beyond.

The 16th century marked the arrival of European explorers, with Portuguese traders sailing along the East African coast. This presence, however, gave way to the dominance of the Omani Arabs, who established control over Zanzibar and the coastal territories, shaping the course of Tanzania's history for centuries to come.

In the late 19th century, the region witnessed the European scramble for Africa, leading to the establishment of German East Africa, which encompassed present-day Tanzania, Rwanda, and Burundi. During this period, German colonization introduced significant changes to the region's governance and infrastructure.

World War I saw German East Africa occupied by British forces, leading to the British administration taking control after the war.

Tanganyika, as it was then called, came under British rule, with administrators implementing various policies, including the introduction of cash crops and infrastructure development.

The 20th century saw a surge in nationalist movements as the people of Tanganyika demanded independence. Led by visionary leaders such as Julius Nyerere, the Tanganyikan independence movement gained momentum, culminating in the country's independence on December 9, 1961. Nyerere became the first Prime Minister and later the President, steering the newly independent nation towards a path of unity, socialism, and self-reliance.

In 1964, Tanganyika merged with Zanzibar, forming the United Republic of Tanzania, as we know it today. The union was a historic moment, uniting the mainland with the archipelago and symbolizing the spirit of African unity.

Over the years, Tanzania has experienced a dynamic political landscape, marked by economic reforms, social progress, and challenges. The nation has navigated through periods of economic growth and setbacks, striving to improve the lives of its people and create a strong sense of national identity.

As we peer into the present, we find a vibrant and diverse nation, boasting a multiplicity of ethnic groups, languages, and cultural traditions. Tanzania's history has been shaped by the interactions of its people, from ancient civilizations and early trade networks to the struggles for independence and the forging of a united nation.

The tapestry of Tanzania's rich history continues to evolve, with each passing moment adding new threads of experiences and achievements. From ancient fossil remains to modern cities, from centuries-old traditions to contemporary innovations, Tanzania's story unfolds as a testament to the resilience and ingenuity of its people. As we embark on this journey through time, let us embrace the depth and complexity of Tanzania's history, cherishing the legacy of the past while looking forward to the promise of the future.

Early Inhabitants and Pre-colonial Cultures

In the ancient tapestry of Tanzania's history, we find the footprints of early inhabitants dating back over two million years. The region's rich archaeological heritage provides us with glimpses into the lives of our ancient ancestors, painting a picture of a land inhabited by early hominids long before recorded history.

The Olduvai Gorge, nestled in northern Tanzania, stands as a treasure trove of fossilized remains and stone tools, revealing the existence of early human beings who once roamed these lands. Pioneering discoveries by archaeologists such as Louis and Mary Leakey have shed light on our evolutionary journey and the ways in which our ancestors adapted to their environment.

As we traverse through time, we encounter the emergence of various indigenous groups, each contributing to the diverse cultural mosaic of Tanzania. The Bantu migration played a pivotal role in shaping the region's cultural landscape, with various Bantu-speaking tribes settling in different parts of the country.

Among these tribes were the ancestors of the Maasai, who are renowned for their pastoral way of life and distinct customs. The Maasai people have preserved their age-old traditions, including their unique dressing style, vibrant beadwork, and age-set systems that govern different life stages.

In the Lake Eyasi region, we encounter the Hadza, one of the last remaining hunter-gatherer communities in Africa. Their ancient lifestyle revolves around foraging for food and living in harmony with nature, providing valuable insights into our prehistoric past.

To the west, the coastal regions of Tanzania bore witness to the rise of Swahili city-states, a civilization influenced by a blend of African, Arab, and Persian cultures. These city-states, such as Kilwa and Sofala, thrived as bustling centers of trade, fostering vibrant cultural exchanges along the Indian Ocean coast.

Throughout the pre-colonial era, trade routes crisscrossed the region, linking the Swahili coast with the interior, facilitating the exchange of goods, ideas, and languages. Swahili, a Bantu language enriched with Arabic loanwords, emerged as a lingua franca and remains a prominent language in Tanzania to this day.

In the central and western parts of Tanzania, the influence of Great Lakes communities, such as the Nyamwezi and Sukuma, contributed to the cultural diversity of the region. These communities were renowned for their agricultural practices, craftsmanship, and traditional beliefs, leaving a lasting impact on Tanzanian culture.

The pre-colonial era also saw the rise of powerful kingdoms, such as the Kingdom of Buganda, located in present-day Uganda, which had significant influence over the neighboring regions, including parts of Tanzania.

In this ancient period, religion played a vital role in the lives of the inhabitants. Indigenous beliefs, animism, and ancestral veneration were prevalent, shaping spiritual practices and rituals that connected people with their environment and ancestors.

As the centuries passed, these diverse cultures intermingled, fostering a rich tapestry of traditions and values that define Tanzania's cultural heritage. The art of storytelling, music, dance, and oral history became integral to passing down knowledge from one generation to another, preserving the essence of Tanzanian identity.

Colonial Era and Struggle for Independence

The colonial era in Tanzania's history marks a significant chapter, characterized by the arrival of European powers seeking to assert control and exploit the region's resources. The 19th century saw the emergence of German and British influence, leaving a lasting impact on the land and its people.

German colonialism in Tanzania began in the late 19th century when Carl Peters, a German explorer, signed treaties with local chiefs, laying claim to vast territories along the East African coast. This marked the establishment of German East Africa, which included present-day Tanzania, Rwanda, and Burundi.

During the German colonial period, the region underwent significant changes, both economically and politically. Germans introduced cash crop plantations, such as coffee and sisal, and established infrastructures like railways, transforming the region's economic landscape.

However, German rule was marked by harsh labor practices, forced labor, and the suppression of local resistance. The "Maji Maji" rebellion, which occurred from 1905 to 1907, was a significant uprising against German colonial rule, led by various ethnic groups who sought to resist the oppressive policies imposed upon them.

With the outbreak of World War I, German East Africa came under attack by British forces from the north and Belgian forces from the west. By 1916, the Germans were defeated, and the British took control of the region, leading to the League of Nations granting Britain a mandate to govern Tanganyika (mainland Tanzania) after the war.

British colonial rule differed from the German administration, with a focus on indirect rule and the promotion of the "civilizing mission." This approach aimed to maintain local authorities while instilling British values and traditions. However, similar to the German era, British rule faced resistance from various nationalist movements seeking self-determination.

The struggle for independence gained momentum in the mid-20th century, fueled by the winds of change sweeping across Africa. Influenced by nationalist ideals and inspired by other African nations achieving independence, Tanganyika's people sought to chart their own destiny.

The Tanganyika African National Union (TANU) emerged as a powerful force, led by the charismatic Julius Nyerere, who would become a prominent figure in Tanzania's history. Nyerere envisioned a united and independent Tanzania, free from colonial rule and discrimination.

Through peaceful and diplomatic means, TANU negotiated with the British authorities, seeking the path to self-governance. On December 9, 1961, Tanganyika gained independence, marking a historic moment in the struggle for freedom and self-determination.

Julius Nyerere became the country's first Prime Minister and later its President, leading Tanzania on a path of socialism, unity, and self-reliance. He advocated the principles of "Ujamaa," a concept emphasizing collective responsibility and communal development.

Zanzibar, too, sought its path to independence, which it achieved on December 10, 1963, becoming a constitutional monarchy under Sultan Jamshid bin Abdullah. However, Zanzibar's independence was short-lived, as a revolution led by Abeid Karume in January 1964 resulted in the overthrow of the Sultanate and the establishment of the People's Republic of Zanzibar.

In April 1964, Tanganyika and Zanzibar unified to form the United Republic of Tanzania, symbolizing the union of the mainland and the archipelago, and creating a diverse and united nation.

Tanzania's struggle for independence was not without challenges, and the nation faced numerous obstacles in its journey towards progress. Yet, through unity, determination, and visionary leadership, Tanzania emerged as an independent nation, free from colonial shackles, and charting its course towards a brighter future.

The Birth of Modern Tanzania: From Tanganyika to the United Republic

As we journey through Tanzania's history, we arrive at a momentous chapter that saw the birth of modern Tanzania, uniting Tanganyika and Zanzibar into the United Republic we know today. This period marked a turning point, shaping the nation's identity and setting the course for its future.

Following Tanganyika's independence from British colonial rule on December 9, 1961, the nation embarked on a path of self-governance under the leadership of its first Prime Minister, Julius Nyerere. Nyerere's vision of a united, socialist, and self-reliant Tanzania guided the young nation towards a brighter future.

Meanwhile, Zanzibar, an archipelago off the coast of Tanzania, also gained independence from British rule on December 10, 1963. Sultan Jamshid bin Abdullah led Zanzibar as a constitutional monarchy, but the struggle for political stability was far from over.

In January 1964, Zanzibar was rocked by a revolution led by Abeid Karume, which resulted in the overthrow of the Sultanate. The revolution sought to address socio-economic disparities and empower the majority African population against the Arab ruling elite. Following the revolution, Zanzibar transformed into the People's Republic of Zanzibar, embracing a new political direction.

The winds of change were blowing across East Africa, and the desire for unity and cooperation between Tanganyika and Zanzibar gained momentum. Leaders from both nations recognized the potential benefits of unification, and discussions began in earnest to forge a strong union.

On April 26, 1964, Tanganyika and Zanzibar officially merged, creating the United Republic of Tanzania. This historic moment symbolized the unification of the mainland and the archipelago, bringing together diverse cultures and traditions under one flag.

Julius Nyerere, a visionary leader known for his pan-Africanist ideals, became the first President of the United Republic of Tanzania. Under his guidance, the nation pursued policies aimed at fostering unity, socialism, and self-reliance.

The Arusha Declaration, delivered by Nyerere on February 5, 1967, laid the foundation for Tanzania's approach to economic and social development. The Declaration emphasized the principles of Ujamaa, promoting collective responsibility and community development, and sought to eliminate inequalities and poverty.

Tanzania's foreign policy under Nyerere's leadership was characterized by non-alignment, emphasizing neutrality in the midst of Cold War tensions. Tanzania played a crucial role in mediating regional conflicts, including brokering peace talks between warring factions in neighboring countries.

In the following years, Tanzania faced various challenges and opportunities. The nation's commitment to education and healthcare saw significant progress, with efforts to increase literacy rates and expand healthcare services to rural communities.

The 1980s saw economic difficulties for Tanzania, leading to the implementation of structural adjustment programs in cooperation with international organizations. These programs aimed to address economic imbalances and improve fiscal stability.

In the early 1990s, Tanzania witnessed political changes as the nation shifted towards multi-party politics. The single-party system was replaced by a multi-party democracy, allowing for a more diverse political landscape.

As Tanzania continued to evolve, the nation maintained a strong sense of cultural pride, celebrating its linguistic diversity, vibrant art, music, and dance, and preserving its rich heritage.

Today, Tanzania stands as a nation with a unique blend of history and progress. From the early struggles for independence to the birth of the United Republic, the nation's journey reflects the resilience and determination of its people. Modern Tanzania embraces its cultural diversity, looks towards economic development, and continues to uphold the ideals of unity and self-reliance.

Exploring Tanzania's Political Landscape

Tanzania's political landscape is as diverse and vibrant as its geographical terrain. From the early days of independence to the present, the nation has witnessed significant political developments that have shaped its governance, policies, and trajectory.

Following Tanganyika's independence in 1961, Julius Nyerere, the visionary leader of the Tanganyika African National Union (TANU), became the country's first Prime Minister. Nyerere's philosophy of Ujamaa, emphasizing communal and collective responsibility, guided the nation's political direction, with a focus on rural development, social welfare, and self-reliance.

In 1962, Tanzania adopted its first constitution, establishing a parliamentary system of government. The Parliament, consisting of the National Assembly and the President, became the supreme law-making body, overseeing the country's legislative affairs.

Tanzania's political landscape experienced significant changes in 1964 when Tanganyika and Zanzibar unified to form the United Republic of Tanzania. This union brought together two distinct political entities, each with its own historical and cultural background. The union aimed to promote unity and solidarity between the mainland and the archipelago.

Julius Nyerere continued to serve as the President of the United Republic, leading Tanzania with a socialist approach and promoting pan-Africanism. His leadership style and commitment to national unity earned him the respect of many both within Tanzania and internationally.

In 1977, Tanzania underwent a significant political transformation with the adoption of a new constitution. This constitution established a one-party state, making the Revolutionary State Party (CCM) the sole legal political party. The one-party system aimed to foster unity and eliminate political divisions that could threaten national cohesion.

Throughout the years, Tanzania's political landscape has witnessed peaceful transitions of power. Following Nyerere's retirement in 1985, Ali Hassan Mwinyi assumed the presidency.

Mwinyi's leadership saw the initiation of economic reforms and the gradual transition towards a market-oriented economy.

In the mid-1990s, Tanzania underwent further political changes as the nation transitioned from a one-party state to a multi-party democracy. The adoption of a new constitution in 1992 paved the way for political pluralism, allowing multiple political parties to participate in the electoral process.

In 1995, Tanzania held its first multi-party elections, and Benjamin Mkapa was elected as the third President of the United Republic. Mkapa's tenure was marked by continued economic reforms and efforts to attract foreign investment.

In 2005, Jakaya Kikwete assumed the presidency after winning the general elections. Kikwete's administration focused on poverty reduction, healthcare, and education, aiming to improve the overall welfare of Tanzanian citizens.

In 2015, Tanzania witnessed a significant political shift with the election of John Pombe Magufuli as the country's fifth President. Magufuli's leadership style earned him the nickname "The Bulldozer" for his zeal in tackling corruption and inefficiency in the government.

Tanzania's political landscape has seen a commitment to peacekeeping and conflict resolution within the region. The nation has played a vital role in mediating conflicts in neighboring countries, demonstrating its dedication to regional stability and cooperation.

Tanzanian Wildlife: A Journey through the Savannah and Beyond

Embark on a thrilling adventure as we venture into the heart of Tanzania's untamed wilderness, where a mesmerizing array of wildlife thrives in its natural habitat. From the vast savannahs to lush forests, Tanzania is a paradise for nature enthusiasts and wildlife lovers alike.

At the forefront of Tanzania's wildlife spectacle stands the legendary Serengeti National Park. This iconic reserve spans over 14,750 square kilometers and hosts one of the most incredible natural phenomena on Earth—the Great Migration. Witness millions of wildebeest, zebras, and other herbivores as they embark on a treacherous journey across the Serengeti in search of greener pastures. The sights and sounds of this majestic migration are awe-inspiring and remain etched in the memory of those lucky enough to witness it.

Venturing into the northern reaches of Tanzania, we find the Ngorongoro Conservation Area, a UNESCO World Heritage Site. At its heart lies the Ngorongoro Crater, a massive caldera formed by a volcanic eruption over two million years ago. This natural enclosure is home to a diverse array of wildlife, including the famed Big Five (lion, elephant, buffalo, leopard, and rhinoceros). The abundant water and vegetation within the crater provide a haven for animals year-round, making it a wildlife enthusiast's dream come true.

As we venture further west, we encounter the lesser-known but equally breathtaking Tarangire National Park. This picturesque reserve, known for its ancient baobab trees and seasonal swamps, hosts an impressive concentration of elephants, making it a popular destination for elephant sightings.

Tanzania's wild wonders extend beyond the savannahs, reaching into the dense forests of Gombe Stream National Park. Made famous by British primatologist Jane Goodall, this park is home to our closest living relatives—the chimpanzees. Spending time with these intelligent and fascinating primates offers an unparalleled glimpse into their social behaviors and complex interactions.

Heading south, we find ourselves in the Selous Game Reserve, one of Africa's largest protected areas. This vast wilderness boasts diverse ecosystems, including woodlands, grasslands, and wetlands. The reserve's immense size allows for the coexistence of numerous species, including elephants, giraffes, lions, and countless bird species.

And let's not forget the picturesque Mount Kilimanjaro, a UNESCO World Heritage Site and the highest peak in Africa. While its snow-capped summit stands as an iconic image, the mountain's slopes and surrounding montane forests are a haven for a variety of wildlife, including colobus monkeys, elephants, and buffalo.

Off the coast of Tanzania lies the marine wonderland of Mafia Island, a marine park with vibrant coral reefs and abundant marine life. Snorkelers and scuba divers can explore the underwater treasures, swimming alongside colorful fish, sea turtles, and even dolphins.

Tanzania's commitment to wildlife conservation is evident through its vast network of protected areas and efforts to combat poaching and habitat destruction. The country's rich biodiversity and commitment to preserving its natural heritage have earned it a reputation as a prime ecotourism destination.

National Parks and Conservation Efforts

In the heart of Tanzania's wild expanse lie the nation's prized possessions—the extraordinary national parks that safeguard its rich biodiversity and natural wonders. Each park tells a unique tale, showcasing the remarkable efforts taken to preserve and protect these precious ecosystems.

The Serengeti National Park, with its sweeping savannahs and awe-inspiring Great Migration, is perhaps the most famous of them all. Designated a UNESCO World Heritage Site, the Serengeti spans thousands of square miles, providing a sanctuary for countless species, including the majestic African lion, graceful cheetah, and elusive leopard.

Adjacent to the Serengeti, we find the Masai Mara National Reserve in Kenya, forming an essential part of the migratory route for wildebeest and zebras. This transboundary ecosystem showcases the significance of cross-border conservation efforts, as animals roam freely between Tanzania and Kenya.

Another iconic national park is the Ngorongoro Conservation Area, encompassing the awe-inspiring Ngorongoro Crater and surrounding highlands. This unique ecosystem hosts a remarkable concentration of wildlife, as animals remain within the crater's boundaries due to its natural enclosure.

Moving south, we encounter the Selous Game Reserve, a sprawling wilderness teeming with an incredible diversity of flora and fauna. Named after British explorer and hunter Frederick Selous, this reserve remains one of the largest protected areas in Africa, providing a haven for elephants, hippos, wild dogs, and much more.

The Tarangire National Park, with its iconic baobab trees and picturesque landscapes, is renowned for its massive elephant herds and numerous bird species. The Tarangire River sustains an abundance of wildlife, making it a wildlife enthusiast's paradise.

In western Tanzania, we discover the vast and remote Mahale Mountains National Park, a sanctuary for chimpanzees and other primates. Trekking through the dense forests to witness these intelligent beings in their natural habitat is an experience like no other.

In the eastern reaches of Tanzania lies the Saadani National Park, where the untamed wilderness meets the Indian Ocean. This unique coastal park allows visitors to witness the rare sight of wildlife near the water's edge, combining a beach experience with a safari adventure.

Tanzania's marine conservation efforts extend beyond the coastline to the islands, including the Zanzibar Archipelago and Mafia Island. The Mafia Island Marine Park and the Menai Bay Conservation Area are protected zones that safeguard the diverse marine life, including endangered species such as sea turtles and dugongs.

The conservation efforts in Tanzania are driven by a dedication to preserving its natural heritage and biodiversity for future generations. The Tanzanian government, along with various non-governmental organizations and international partners, actively participates in protecting these pristine environments from poaching, habitat loss, and other threats.

One of the country's visionary conservation initiatives is the establishment of community-based conservation projects. These projects involve local communities in wildlife management, creating a sense of ownership and responsibility. By involving the people who live in close proximity to these protected areas, the efforts to conserve the wildlife and habitats become more effective and sustainable.

The success of these conservation efforts is evident in the growth of animal populations, such as elephants and rhinos, in various parks. The government's commitment to anti-poaching initiatives, strict wildlife protection laws, and international collaborations has resulted in a decline in illegal wildlife trade and poaching activities.

Tanzania's national parks and conservation efforts serve as a beacon of hope for preserving Africa's wildlife and natural heritage. These protected areas not only provide sanctuary for countless species but also contribute to the nation's ecotourism industry, supporting local communities and promoting awareness about the importance of wildlife conservation.

Discovering the Unique Flora and Fauna of Tanzania

From the vast savannahs to the lush forests and breathtaking marine ecosystems, Tanzania is a treasure trove of biodiversity that never fails to amaze and inspire. Let's begin our journey in the renowned Serengeti National Park, where the iconic African lion reigns as the king of the savannah. Roaming alongside them are agile cheetahs, elusive leopards, and powerful African elephants. The Great Migration, a spectacle like no other, showcases millions of wildebeests and zebras on their epic quest for greener pastures, painting the landscape with a mesmerizing display of movement and sound.

Moving to the Ngorongoro Conservation Area, we encounter the stunning Ngorongoro Crater, a unique caldera hosting an array of wildlife. Here, the endangered black rhino finds refuge, alongside the awe-inspiring African buffalo, graceful Grant's gazelle, and vibrant flamingos that grace the soda lakes with their presence.

Tanzania's southern parks, like Ruaha National Park, are a haven for diverse species. The park's rugged terrain and vast river systems harbor large populations of lions, leopards, and elephants, along with the elusive African wild dog, whose fascinating social structure sets it apart from other predators.

Venturing westward, the Mahale Mountains National Park beckons with its dense forests and tranquil shores of Lake Tanganyika. Among the verdant vegetation reside chimpanzees, with whom visitors can engage in a unique and immersive wildlife encounter.

The eastern coast of Tanzania boasts the Saadani National Park, where pristine beaches meet untamed wilderness. Here, visitors can catch glimpses of rare marine species, such as the Indo-Pacific humpback dolphins and endangered green turtles, basking in the warm coastal waters.

Tanzania's marine wonders extend further to the Zanzibar Archipelago and Mafia Island, where vibrant coral reefs and teeming marine life await. Snorkelers and scuba divers can explore the underwater realm, swimming alongside majestic manta rays, curious reef sharks, and an array of colorful reef fish.

The unique baobab trees dotting the landscape of the Tarangire National Park form an iconic backdrop for an array of wildlife. In addition to large elephant herds, the park is home to the fringed-eared oryx, rare tree-climbing lions, and the distinctive long-necked gerenuk.

Not to be overlooked are the lesser-known gems, such as the Katavi National Park in western Tanzania. This remote and untouched wilderness offers a glimpse of Africa as it once was, with vast herds of buffalo, crocodile-infested rivers, and the awe-inspiring sight of hippos crowding in shrinking waterholes.

Tanzania's floral diversity is equally breathtaking, with over 11,000 plant species identified across the nation. From the towering baobabs to the delicate orchids, the flora contributes to the complex ecosystem that sustains the diverse fauna.

The country's numerous lakes and wetlands, like Lake Victoria and the Rufiji River Delta, provide crucial habitats for an assortment of bird species. Over 1,100 bird species have been recorded in Tanzania, making it a birdwatcher's paradise.

Conservation efforts in Tanzania have been instrumental in preserving these incredible ecosystems and protecting the unique flora and fauna. The establishment of national parks, community-based conservation projects, and anti-poaching initiatives play a pivotal role in safeguarding the nation's natural heritage.

Culinary Traditions of the Tanzanian Table

Prepare to embark on a delightful gastronomic journey through the rich and diverse culinary traditions of Tanzania. Just as the nation's landscape is a tapestry of contrasts, so too is its cuisine—a harmonious blend of indigenous flavors, cultural influences, and regional specialties that come together to create a symphony of taste sensations.

At the heart of Tanzanian cuisine lies a staple that nourishes the nation—the beloved ugali. This maize-based dish, similar to polenta, forms the backbone of many meals, served alongside a variety of flavorful accompaniments. Ugali is the epitome of communal dining, often shared from a communal bowl as a gesture of unity and togetherness.

In the coastal regions, the influence of Arabic and Indian cultures adds a unique twist to Tanzanian fare. Spices like cardamom, cloves, and cinnamon infuse dishes with a burst of flavor, elevating everyday meals to culinary delights. The coastal areas are also famous for their delicious seafood, with dishes like coconut-infused curries and grilled fish tantalizing taste buds.

Venturing inland, the Swahili-inspired cuisine blends the flavors of Africa and the Arab world. Pilau, a fragrant rice dish seasoned with spices, is a staple on many Swahili tables, while biryani, a dish of rice cooked with meat or vegetables and aromatic spices, is a must-try for visitors seeking a flavorful culinary adventure.

In the mountainous regions, you'll discover hearty stews and broths, brimming with locally sourced vegetables and tender chunks of meat. One such dish is mtori, a delicious green banana and beef stew, bursting with rich and savory flavors.

The Maasai people, renowned for their pastoral way of life, contribute to Tanzania's culinary tapestry with their unique dishes. One such delicacy is nyama choma, succulent grilled meat seasoned with simple but flavorful marinades, often served at gatherings and celebrations.

Tanzania's proximity to the Indian Ocean also brings forth a mouthwatering array of seafood delights. Freshly caught fish, prawns, and squid find their way onto plates, often prepared with coconut milk, chili, and lime to create a symphony of tastes that celebrate the ocean's bounty.

For the adventurous foodie, Tanzania offers a taste of the wild with dishes like kongoro, a tasty dish made from roasted grasshoppers, enjoyed as a crunchy and protein-rich snack in some regions.

When it comes to street food, Tanzanian markets come alive with an assortment of delectable treats. Sambusas, similar to Indian samosas, are popular street snacks filled with meat, vegetables, or lentils and seasoned with aromatic spices. Mandazis, delightful fried dough snacks, are perfect for satisfying midday cravings.

No culinary journey through Tanzania would be complete without indulging in a cup of chai—spiced tea that warms the soul and brings people together for lively conversations and shared moments of joy.

Tanzanian culinary traditions are not just about the food but also about the communal experience. The act of sharing a meal, whether with family, friends, or strangers, is a cherished tradition that fosters a sense of togetherness and unity.

Savoring the Delicacies of Swahili Cuisine

At the heart of Swahili cuisine lies a love for spices. Cinnamon, cloves, cardamom, and cumin infuse dishes with a warm and aromatic essence, transforming ordinary ingredients into culinary masterpieces. The use of these spices harks back to the historical trade routes that connected the Swahili Coast to distant lands, allowing for the exchange of goods and flavors that continue to influence the cuisine today.

One of the signature dishes of Swahili cuisine is pilau, a fragrant rice dish that boasts a tantalizing blend of spices, meat, and vegetables. Served at special occasions and everyday gatherings alike, pilau is a dish that brings people together, uniting them in the joy of savoring its complex flavors.

Another culinary gem is biryani, a dish of flavorful rice cooked with meat or vegetables, often served at weddings and festive celebrations. This aromatic delight is a testament to the Arab and Indian influences that have shaped Swahili cuisine, as the dish arrived on the Swahili Coast through centuries of cultural exchange.

In coastal towns, seafood reigns supreme, and Swahili cuisine celebrates the bounty of the Indian Ocean. From sumptuous grilled fish seasoned with coconut and lime to rich coconut-infused curries with prawns and squid, the coastal flavors transport diners to a culinary paradise by the sea.

Zanzibar, an integral part of the Swahili Coast, adds its own unique flavors to the mix. The island is famous for its tantalizing street food, such as mishkaki, succulent skewered meat marinated in a spicy sauce, and urojo, a flavorful soup made with lentils, potatoes, and coconut milk.

For those with a sweet tooth, Zanzibar's delightful treats include mkate wa kumimina, a coconut and cardamom-flavored pancake that is both crispy and chewy, and halua, a delicious semolina and coconut pudding infused with aromatic spices.

As we savor the delicacies of Swahili cuisine, we are invited to explore the essence of the Swahili culture—a tapestry of diverse influences that have come together to create a truly unique culinary experience. The act of sharing a meal, whether with family or friends, is at the heart of Swahili hospitality, and it is through these shared moments that the flavors and traditions of Swahili cuisine come alive.

Swahili cuisine is a celebration of cultural diversity and the power of food to bring people together, transcending borders and uniting hearts. With every bite, we savor the essence of centuries of history, trade, and cultural exchange, reminding us that the joy of food is not just in its taste but in the stories it tells and the memories it creates.

Zanzibar: A Spice-infused Paradise

Zanzibar's rich history is intertwined with its spice trade, earning it the nickname "The Spice Island." For centuries, this tropical gem has been a hub for the cultivation and export of spices that have tantalized the palates of people across the world.

As you wander through the narrow streets of Stone Town, the historic heart of Zanzibar, you'll be greeted by a whirlwind of scents emanating from spice markets and local food stalls. Here, you can sample an array of spices, from cloves and cinnamon to cardamom and nutmeg, which have been at the core of Zanzibar's prosperity and cultural identity.

The spice plantations that dot the island's lush interior offer an immersive experience into the world of spice cultivation. Guided tours take you on a sensory adventure, allowing you to touch, smell, and taste the spices in their natural habitat. Discover how cloves, one of the most sought-after spices, are carefully harvested and dried under the tropical sun, infusing the air with their aromatic essence.

Vanilla, another prized spice, is hand-pollinated by skilled farmers, making Zanzibar one of the few places in the world where this labor-intensive process is still practiced. The result is some of the finest and most flavorful vanilla in the world, a true treasure of the island.

But Zanzibar's allure goes beyond its spice heritage. The island boasts some of the world's most breathtaking beaches, with powdery white sands and crystal-clear waters that beckon travelers to unwind and bask in the warm tropical sun. Diving and snorkeling enthusiasts can explore the vibrant coral reefs, teeming with colorful marine life, including playful dolphins and graceful sea turtles.

For history buffs, Zanzibar offers a glimpse into its rich cultural past, evident in the intricate architecture of Stone Town. The blend of Swahili, Arabic, and European influences is evident in the ornate wooden doors, narrow alleyways, and historical landmarks that narrate the island's fascinating past as a trading post and melting pot of cultures.

Zanzibar's cuisine is as diverse as its cultural heritage. From delectable seafood dishes infused with aromatic spices to mouthwatering coconut-based curries, every meal is a celebration of flavor and tradition. Don't forget to try the Zanzibari pizza, a unique street food that fuses local and international flavors in a delightful culinary creation.

As the sun sets over the horizon, the island comes alive with vibrant nightlife. Live music, traditional dance performances, and bustling night markets add to the island's allure, providing visitors with a taste of the local rhythms and vibrant energy.

Zanzibar's warmth extends beyond its tropical climate; it lies in the genuine hospitality of its people, who welcome visitors with open arms and radiant smiles. The Swahili culture's spirit of "karibu," which means "welcome" in Swahili, permeates every interaction, making visitors feel at home in this exotic paradise.

Whether you're seeking a tranquil retreat, an adventure-filled getaway, or a cultural exploration, Zanzibar has it all. This spice-infused paradise leaves an indelible mark on those who visit, capturing their hearts with its sensory delights, rich history, and warm embrace.

Experiencing Wildlife Safaris: The Tanzanian Safari Magic

Imagine yourself in an open safari vehicle, surrounded by the vast African savannah, as the golden sun rises and bathes the landscape in its warm glow. You take a deep breath, inhaling the fresh scent of the wild, and in that moment, you know you are about to embark on an extraordinary journey—the magic of a Tanzanian wildlife safari.

Tanzania, with its diverse and pristine landscapes, is a safari enthusiast's dream come true. It is home to some of the world's most iconic and abundant wildlife, making it a prime destination for those seeking an unforgettable encounter with the animal kingdom.

The Serengeti National Park, with its endless plains and teeming wildlife, stands as the epitome of a Tanzanian safari experience. Here, you'll witness the awe-inspiring Great Migration, where millions of wildebeests, zebras, and other herbivores traverse the plains in search of fresh grazing grounds, pursued by predators like lions and cheetahs. The sight of this natural spectacle is nothing short of breathtaking, a display of nature's grandeur that leaves you in awe of the circle of life.

Moving to the Ngorongoro Conservation Area, you'll encounter the Ngorongoro Crater, a caldera that shelters a remarkable concentration of wildlife within its natural amphitheater. This UNESCO World Heritage Site is a haven for the Big Five—lion, elephant, buffalo, leopard, and rhinoceros. As you gaze into the crater, you'll witness a microcosm of African wildlife coexisting harmoniously, a testament to the delicate balance of nature.

Further west, the Tarangire National Park unfolds before your eyes, with its ancient baobab trees and the Tarangire River serving as a vital water source for the resident wildlife. The park is famed for its large herds of elephants, and you'll be captivated by the sight of these majestic creatures as they quench their thirst and frolic in the water.

Heading south, you'll encounter the Selous Game Reserve, one of Africa's largest protected areas and a UNESCO World Heritage

Site. This vast wilderness is a sanctuary for a plethora of species, including elephants, lions, giraffes, and countless bird species. The meandering Rufiji River, with its lagoons and sandbanks, offers a unique opportunity to spot hippos, crocodiles, and water birds in their natural habitat.

In the western reaches of Tanzania, you'll find the remote and untouched beauty of the Katavi National Park. Here, you'll witness vast herds of buffalo gathering around dwindling waterholes, while the skies are filled with flocks of birds migrating across the landscape.

For an entirely different safari experience, venture to the Gombe Stream National Park, where the focus shifts from the savannah to the dense forests. This park is renowned for its chimpanzee population, offering an intimate and immersive encounter with our closest living relatives. Observing the playful interactions and social dynamics of these intelligent primates is a memory that will stay with you forever.

Tanzanian safari guides are not just experts in tracking wildlife; they are storytellers, narrating the tales of the animal kingdom with passion and knowledge. Their expertise, honed from years of experience, ensures that every safari is a thrilling and informative adventure, filled with fascinating insights into the behavior and ecology of the animals you encounter.

But the magic of a Tanzanian safari extends beyond the wildlife sightings. It is the feeling of being a part of this untamed world, where nature reigns supreme, and humans are merely observers in the grand theater of life. It is the quiet moments, when you pause to absorb the sounds of the wilderness—the distant roar of a lion, the haunting calls of a hyena, or the gentle rustle of leaves—that stir a deep connection with nature and remind us of our place in the natural order.

The responsible tourism practices embraced by Tanzania ensure that wildlife conservation remains a top priority. Efforts to combat poaching, protect habitats, and promote sustainable practices make Tanzania a leader in wildlife conservation.

Exploring Serengeti National Park: A Wildlife Spectacle

The Serengeti is best known for the Great Migration—an awe-inspiring journey undertaken by millions of wildebeests, zebras, and gazelles as they traverse the vast savannah in search of fresh grazing grounds. This mesmerizing migration is a sight to behold, captivating both wildlife enthusiasts and nature photographers alike. The thundering hooves of the herbivores, accompanied by the guttural roars of lions and the stealthy strides of cheetahs, create a symphony of life that reverberates across the plains.

The cycle of the Great Migration is a continuous spectacle that follows the seasonal rhythm of the Serengeti. From December to April, the southern Serengeti is dotted with newborn calves, as the wildebeest give birth to their young during the calving season. This period attracts predators like lions, leopards, and hyenas, who seize the opportunity to feast on the vulnerable young. It is a delicate dance of life and death that sustains the circle of life in this wild wonderland.

As the dry season sets in from May to July, the herds start their arduous journey northward in search of greener pastures. The iconic river crossings over the crocodile-infested Mara River become a highlight of the migration. Witnessing the bravery and determination of the animals as they navigate the treacherous waters is a humbling experience, evoking a deep appreciation for their resilience.

From July to October, the northern Serengeti becomes the stage for one of the most dramatic parts of the migration—the Grumeti River crossing. This is a time of high drama and intense action, as the herds face the formidable task of traversing the river, often falling victim to the lurking crocodiles. Yet, this perilous journey is vital for their survival, as the lush grasses of the Maasai Mara in Kenya await them on the other side.

Beyond the Great Migration, the Serengeti teems with wildlife year-round. The Big Five—lion, elephant, buffalo, leopard, and rhinoceros—roam freely in this protected sanctuary. The Serengeti is a haven for cheetahs, whose speed and agility make them formidable hunters, and elusive leopards, masters of stealth who prowl the treetops in search of prey.

Birdwatchers are in for a treat in the Serengeti, as over 500 bird species call this paradise home. From the vibrant lilac-breasted roller to the majestic African fish eagle, each bird adds its own melody to the symphony of the Serengeti.

The vastness of the Serengeti allows for a variety of safari experiences. Game drives in open safari vehicles offer unparalleled opportunities to observe wildlife up close, while hot air balloon safaris provide a unique perspective, allowing visitors to witness the Serengeti from the skies as the sun rises over the horizon.

The Serengeti's conservation efforts are crucial to preserving this pristine ecosystem. The Tanzanian government, in partnership with various conservation organizations, actively works to protect the park from poaching and habitat loss. Sustainable tourism practices also play a vital role in ensuring the long-term preservation of the Serengeti's biodiversity.

Every visit to the Serengeti is a pilgrimage to the untamed heart of Africa. It is a place where the ancient rhythms of the natural world still beat strong, reminding us of the intricate web of life that connects all living beings. The Serengeti's beauty, splendor, and raw power leave an indelible mark on all who venture into its wilderness, evoking a profound sense of wonder and appreciation for the rich tapestry of life that thrives here.

Ngorongoro Crater: Nature's Sunken Paradise

Hidden within the highlands of northern Tanzania lies a natural wonder unlike any other—the Ngorongoro Crater. This breathtaking caldera, formed millions of years ago by the collapse of a massive volcano, is nature's sunken paradise, a haven for a remarkable concentration of wildlife and a testament to the incredible power of geology.

As you descend into the Ngorongoro Crater, you are enveloped by a world of unparalleled beauty—a vast expanse of grasslands, acacia woodlands, and shimmering soda lakes cradled by steep walls that rise over 2,000 feet above sea level. This unique topography creates a natural enclosure, providing a sanctuary for an astonishing array of animals.

The Ngorongoro Crater is renowned for its diverse wildlife population, earning it the title of "Africa's Eden." Within this 100-square-mile expanse, the Big Five—lion, elephant, buffalo, leopard, and rhinoceros—roam freely, as if part of a living tapestry woven by nature itself.

The grassy plains, dotted with herds of wildebeests, zebras, and gazelles, serve as prime grazing grounds for these herbivores. As they graze, they unwittingly provide sustenance for the predators that lurk in the shadows, such as lions and cheetahs, who lie in wait for the perfect moment to strike.

Ngorongoro's rhinoceros population is a particular highlight, as it is one of the few places in Tanzania where you can spot these elusive creatures in the wild. Both the black rhinoceros and the white rhinoceros find refuge in this protected sanctuary, providing visitors with a rare opportunity to witness these endangered giants up close.

Bird enthusiasts will find their haven in the Ngorongoro Crater as well, with over 500 avian species gracing the skies. From vibrant flamingos wading in the soda lakes to regal African fish eagles perched in the acacia trees, the birdlife adds an enchanting dimension to the already vibrant landscape.

The cradle of life in Ngorongoro extends beyond the land to the waters of Lake Magadi, a soda lake that shimmers like a mirage amidst the golden savannah. The lake supports a thriving ecosystem of birdlife, including flocks of pink-hued lesser flamingos, who paint the waters with their elegant presence.

Beyond its wildlife wonders, the Ngorongoro Crater also holds significant archaeological importance. The Olduvai Gorge, located within the crater, is considered one of the most important paleoanthropological sites in the world. Fossilized remains of early human ancestors and ancient hominid footprints dating back millions of years have been unearthed here, providing invaluable insights into the origins of humankind.

Conservation efforts play a crucial role in preserving the delicate balance of life within the Ngorongoro Crater. The Tanzanian government, in collaboration with conservation organizations, works diligently to protect the park from poaching and habitat destruction, ensuring that future generations can continue to marvel at the wonders of this natural paradise.

The Maasai people, who have inhabited the surrounding lands for centuries, also play a significant role in the conservation of the Ngorongoro Crater. They coexist harmoniously with the wildlife, practicing traditional livestock herding while respecting the delicate ecosystem that sustains both their communities and the animals that call this sunken paradise home.

A visit to the Ngorongoro Crater is a journey into the heart of a timeless sanctuary—a living testament to the majesty of nature and the resilience of the animals that thrive here. As you gaze upon the sweeping vistas and the intimate wildlife encounters, you are reminded of the interconnectedness of all living beings and the need to cherish and protect our planet's natural wonders.

The Wonders of Selous Game Reserve

Selous is a wilderness of superlatives, home to an unparalleled diversity of wildlife and landscapes that will leave you in awe. As you venture into this vast and remote wilderness, you are greeted by a panorama of untamed beauty—rolling savannahs, riverine forests, and meandering waterways that support an extraordinary variety of species.

The Rufiji River, the lifeblood of Selous, snakes its way through the reserve, creating a tapestry of lush wetlands and marshes that teem with birdlife and wildlife. It is one of Africa's most significant rivers, a lifeline for the myriad animals that rely on its waters for survival.

The Selous is a haven for the Big Five, and you'll have the opportunity to encounter these iconic animals in their natural habitat. Lions, with their majestic manes, rule the savannahs, while herds of elephants, the gentle giants of Africa, amble gracefully along the riverbanks. Buffaloes roam in large numbers, forming formidable herds that shape the ecosystem, while elusive leopards, masters of stealth, survey their territory from the treetops.

The reserve is also famous for its thriving wild dog population—the African wild dogs, also known as painted wolves. These highly social and intelligent predators form close-knit packs, cooperating in a strategic hunt that ensures their survival. Observing these rare and endangered animals in the wild is a privilege that few have the chance to experience.

Selous is a paradise for birdwatchers, with over 440 bird species recorded in the reserve. From the vibrant lilac-breasted roller to the majestic African fish eagle, every bird adds its own melody to the symphony of the Selous. The Rufiji River delta is particularly renowned for attracting a dazzling array of water birds, providing a visual feast for bird enthusiasts.

The beauty of Selous lies not only in its wildlife but also in its sense of untouched wilderness. Unlike many other national parks and reserves, Selous allows for a more intimate and exclusive safari experience. The reserve's vastness and limited number of visitors ensure that you can immerse yourself in the serenity of nature without the crowds.

Selous is also a haven for water-based safaris, offering a unique perspective on the wildlife and landscapes. Boat safaris along the Rufiji River provide a front-row seat to the ever-changing drama of the animal kingdom—a chance to witness elephants bathing, hippos basking in the sun, and crocodiles patrolling the riverbanks.

In addition to game drives and boat safaris, walking safaris are a signature experience in Selous. Accompanied by expert guides, you'll step into the heart of the wilderness, where you can appreciate the smaller details of the ecosystem and feel a deep connection to nature.

Selous Game Reserve is a model of conservation and sustainable tourism. It remains one of the least visited parks in Tanzania, ensuring that its pristine ecosystems are preserved for future generations. Conservation efforts, including anti-poaching patrols and community engagement, are crucial in safeguarding this natural wonder.

The Selous Game Reserve is more than just a destination—it is an experience that leaves an indelible mark on your soul. The untamed beauty, the thrill of wildlife encounters, and the sense of being immersed in a vast and timeless wilderness create memories that last a lifetime.

Mount Kilimanjaro: Scaling Africa's Tallest Peak

Mount Kilimanjaro stands as a majestic sentinel, rising proudly from the plains of Tanzania to claim its title as Africa's tallest peak. This iconic volcanic mountain, with its snow-capped summit, has long captured the imagination of adventurers and explorers from all corners of the globe.

Towering at an impressive 19,341 feet (5,895 meters) above sea level, Mount Kilimanjaro's summit, known as Uhuru Peak, is a beacon of challenge and triumph. Scaling this mighty mountain is a feat that attracts thousands of climbers each year, all seeking to conquer its heights and stand on the rooftop of Africa. But Kilimanjaro is not just any mountain; it is a unique wonder of nature. Classified as a dormant stratovolcano, Kilimanjaro is comprised of three distinct volcanic cones: Kibo, Mawenzi, and Shira. Kibo is the highest and hosts Uhuru Peak, while Mawenzi and Shira are the other two cones that add to the mountain's majestic profile.

One of the most intriguing aspects of Mount Kilimanjaro is its ecological diversity. It encompasses five distinct ecological zones, each with its own unique flora and fauna. Starting from the cultivated farmlands at the mountain's base, climbers ascend through the lush montane forest, home to a variety of plants and animals, including elusive monkeys and colorful bird species.

As climbers continue their ascent, they enter the heath and moorland zone, a landscape characterized by rolling hills, rocky terrain, and intriguing plant species like the giant groundsel and lobelia. This zone gives way to the highland desert, where the air thins, and the landscape becomes barren and lunar-like, with little vegetation to be seen. Finally, as climbers reach the alpine desert, they encounter the breathtaking glaciers and snowfields that crown the summit. These glaciers have been steadily retreating over the years, and there are ongoing efforts to study and monitor their changes due to climate change.

Climbing Mount Kilimanjaro requires physical and mental endurance, but it does not necessitate technical mountaineering skills. As a result, Kilimanjaro is often referred to as the

"Everyman's Everest." Climbers need determination, perseverance, and the ability to adapt to changing altitudes and weather conditions. There are several routes to reach the summit, each offering a different experience and level of difficulty. The Marangu route, also known as the "Coca-Cola route," is one of the more popular routes, featuring hut accommodations along the way. The Machame route, known as the "Whiskey route," is another popular choice, offering stunning views and a diverse landscape.

The Lemosho and Northern Circuit routes are gaining popularity due to their longer itineraries, allowing for better acclimatization and higher chances of success in reaching the summit. For those seeking a more challenging and less frequented route, the Rongai and Umbwe routes are excellent options.

Climbers must be aware of the potential risks associated with ascending Kilimanjaro, including altitude sickness. Acclimatization is critical to ensure a successful summit attempt and the well-being of climbers. Experienced guides and porters play a crucial role in supporting climbers on their journey and ensuring their safety throughout the expedition.

As climbers approach the summit, they are often greeted by a breathtaking sunrise—the legendary "Kilimanjaro sunrise." Standing on the roof of Africa, looking out over the vast African plains, is an experience that evokes a sense of triumph, humility, and connection with nature.

Kilimanjaro's allure extends beyond the climbers who conquer its heights. The mountain holds cultural significance for the local Chagga people, who inhabit the slopes and have lived in harmony with Kilimanjaro for generations. The mountain's name itself is believed to be derived from the Swahili phrase "Kilima Njaro," meaning "shining mountain" or "white mountain."

As climbers descend back to the base, they carry with them memories of a lifetime—a journey of self-discovery, camaraderie, and the triumph of human spirit over nature's grand challenges. Scaling Africa's tallest peak is not just a physical endeavor; it is a profound and transformative experience—a testament to the power of human determination and a celebration of the natural wonders that grace our planet.

The Stunning Beauty of Lake Victoria

Nestled in the heart of East Africa, Lake Victoria is a stunning gem that captivates with its vastness and natural splendor. As the largest tropical lake in the world, Lake Victoria spans over 26,000 square miles, making it one of the planet's most significant freshwater bodies.

The lake is shared by three East African countries—Tanzania, Uganda, and Kenya—with the majority of its waters belonging to Tanzania and Uganda. Lake Victoria serves as a vital resource for the surrounding communities, providing water for drinking, agriculture, and fishing.

The beauty of Lake Victoria lies not only in its size but also in its diverse and rich ecosystem. The lake is teeming with life, from the myriad fish species that call its waters home to the countless bird species that grace its shores. With its lush islands, dense papyrus swamps, and serene bays, Lake Victoria creates a haven for a remarkable array of flora and fauna.

The lake's shorelines are alive with the calls of various bird species, including the African fish eagle, whose distinctive cry resonates across the waters. From colorful kingfishers to graceful herons, birdwatchers are treated to a visual feast as they explore the lake's rich birdlife.

The waters of Lake Victoria are home to hundreds of fish species, with the most famous being the Nile perch. This large predator was introduced to the lake in the 1950s and has since become a significant part of the region's fishing industry. However, the introduction of the Nile perch has also had ecological consequences, affecting native fish populations and leading to concerns about conservation.

Fishing on Lake Victoria is not just a livelihood; it is also an integral part of the region's culture and traditions. Local communities have relied on the lake's resources for generations, and fishing remains a way of life for many who inhabit its shores. However, sustainable fishing practices are crucial to ensure the lake's long-term health and the preservation of its biodiversity.

The islands that dot the surface of Lake Victoria are an essential part of its charm. From the Ssese Islands in Uganda to the Ukara

Island in Tanzania, these islands offer tranquil retreats and opportunities for ecotourism. Visitors can immerse themselves in the local culture, explore lush forests, and witness stunning sunsets over the glistening waters.

Lake Victoria's strategic location has also played a significant role in shaping the region's history and economy. The lake serves as a vital transport route, connecting the East African countries and facilitating trade and commerce. Ferries and boats ply the waters, carrying passengers and goods between towns and islands, fostering connections and community ties.

Despite its beauty and importance, Lake Victoria faces environmental challenges. Pollution, overfishing, and invasive species threaten the delicate balance of its ecosystem. Conservation efforts, however, are underway to protect the lake's biodiversity and safeguard its future for generations to come.

The stunning beauty of Lake Victoria is not just confined to its waters and islands. The lake's sunsets are legendary, painting the sky with vibrant hues that reflect upon the water's surface. The sight of fishermen's boats silhouetted against the setting sun creates a timeless scene, evoking a sense of peace and serenity.

Lake Victoria's allure extends beyond its natural wonders. The warmth and hospitality of the people who call its shores home add a special touch to any visit. Exploring the local communities and immersing oneself in their culture is a transformative experience that fosters a deeper understanding of the lake's significance in their lives.

Zanzibar Archipelago: Tropical Paradise Found

The Zanzibar Archipelago comprises several islands, with the two main ones being Unguja, commonly known as Zanzibar Island, and Pemba Island. These islands are surrounded by smaller islets that add to the archipelago's allure, such as Mnemba Island, Chumbe Island, and Prison Island, each offering its unique charm and appeal.

The island of Unguja, Zanzibar's main attraction, boasts a rich history and cultural heritage. Stone Town, a UNESCO World Heritage Site and the historic heart of Zanzibar City, is a labyrinth of narrow streets, ancient buildings, and bustling markets that hark back to a bygone era. Here, you'll find ornate wooden doors, quaint cafes, and lively bazaars selling spices, textiles, and traditional crafts.

Zanzibar's history is intertwined with the spice trade, and its aromatic legacy lives on. The Spice Tour, a popular excursion, takes visitors on a sensory journey through spice plantations, where they can experience the scents and flavors of cloves, nutmeg, cinnamon, and more. This is a chance to learn about the island's spice industry, which has been a significant part of its identity for centuries.

The island's diverse cultural influences are evident in its cuisine. Zanzibari food is a delightful fusion of Arabic, Indian, African, and Portuguese flavors, resulting in a delectable blend of spices and aromas. From the mouthwatering seafood dishes to the flavorful pilau rice and mouthwatering Zanzibar pizza, the island's culinary scene is a treat for the senses.

But perhaps Zanzibar's most alluring feature is its stunning coastline. Miles of palm-fringed, white sandy beaches stretch along the island's shores, caressed by the crystal-clear waters of the Indian Ocean. Snorkeling and diving enthusiasts are drawn to Zanzibar's rich marine life, with opportunities to explore vibrant coral reefs teeming with tropical fish, dolphins, and even the occasional encounter with gentle whale sharks.

The northern tip of Zanzibar is home to the legendary Nungwi Beach, known for its idyllic beauty and sunset views. Here, you can indulge in beachside relaxation, water sports, and sailing trips aboard traditional dhows, the iconic sailboats that have been used for centuries along the East African coast.

At the southern end of the island lies the serene Jambiani Beach, where the pace of life slows to a gentle rhythm. This is a place to experience the simple pleasures of beachcombing, watching fishermen at work, and savoring the tranquility of the ocean's embrace.

For those seeking a dose of adventure, the neighboring island of Pemba offers a more off-the-beaten-path experience. Pemba is known for its lush forests, abundant marine life, and diving opportunities that rival those of its more famous neighbor. Here, you can explore ancient ruins, swim in the mangrove forests, and witness traditional boat-making crafts.

The Zanzibar Archipelago's beauty extends beyond its shores to the warm hospitality of its people. The islanders, known as Zanzibaris, welcome visitors with open arms and a genuine smile, embodying the spirit of "Karibu"—Swahili for "welcome." Engaging with the locals and learning about their way of life is an enriching aspect of any Zanzibar journey.

As the sun dips below the horizon, painting the sky with hues of gold and pink, you can't help but be enchanted by the magic of the Zanzibar Archipelago. It is a place of wonder, where the beauty of nature and the warmth of the local culture come together to create an unforgettable experience.

Stone Town: A Journey Back in Time

Step into the captivating world of Stone Town—a place where time seems to stand still, and the echoes of history resonate through every narrow alleyway and ancient building. This UNESCO World Heritage Site, located on the island of Unguja in Zanzibar, is a living testament to the rich cultural heritage and storied past of the Zanzibari people.

As you wander through the labyrinth of winding streets and alleys, you are transported back in time to a bygone era—a time when Stone Town was a thriving center of trade and cultural exchange, drawing merchants, explorers, and adventurers from distant lands.

Stone Town's architecture is a reflection of the diverse influences that have shaped its identity over the centuries. The ornate wooden doors that grace many buildings are a hallmark of Swahili craftsmanship, each door telling its own story through intricately carved designs and motifs.

The town's buildings display a blend of Arabic, Indian, European, and African architectural styles, creating a unique and harmonious tapestry of cultures. From the imposing Arab Fort, with its sturdy coral stone walls, to the elegant House of Wonders, which once served as the Sultan's palace, Stone Town's buildings are a visual delight, reminiscent of a time when Zanzibar was a thriving center of commerce and power.

The heart of Stone Town is its bustling marketplaces, where the vibrant colors and aromas of spices, fruits, and textiles fill the air. The Darajani Market, in particular, is a sensory delight, offering an authentic glimpse into the daily life of the Zanzibari people. Here, locals and visitors alike can shop for fresh produce, sample street food delights, and experience the lively atmosphere of a traditional East African market.

One of Stone Town's most iconic features is its seafront, which offers sweeping views of the Indian Ocean. The Forodhani Gardens, a popular gathering spot for locals and tourists alike, come alive in the evening with food stalls selling Zanzibar's famous street food, including Zanzibar pizza, grilled seafood, and sugarcane juice.

Beyond its architectural beauty and bustling markets, Stone Town is a place of historical significance. The town played a central role in the East African slave trade during the 19th century, and visitors can learn about this dark chapter of history at the Slave Chambers, where enslaved individuals were held before being transported to other parts of the world.

Stone Town is also a hub of cultural expression, with art galleries, craft shops, and cultural centers showcasing the work of local artists and artisans. Traditional music and dance performances are held regularly, providing visitors with an opportunity to experience the vibrant rhythms and movements that are an integral part of Zanzibari culture.

The town's narrow streets and alleys are an invitation to get lost and explore, stumbling upon hidden gems such as quaint cafes, boutique hotels, and art studios. Every corner of Stone Town has a story to tell, and its residents are eager to share the tales of their beloved town.

Stone Town's charm lies not just in its historical landmarks but also in the warmth and hospitality of its people. Zanzibaris are known for their friendliness and their eagerness to welcome visitors into their community. Engaging with the locals and learning about their traditions and way of life is an enriching aspect of any visit to Stone Town.

As the sun sets over the horizon, casting a warm glow over the ancient buildings, you can't help but feel a sense of wonder and reverence for Stone Town—a place that has stood the test of time and remains a living tribute to the rich tapestry of history and culture that has shaped Zanzibar's identity.

Dar es Salaam: Tanzania's Thriving Metropolis

Welcome to Dar es Salaam, the bustling and vibrant metropolis that serves as Tanzania's commercial and cultural heart. This coastal city, whose name means "Haven of Peace" in Arabic, is a captivating blend of old-world charm and modern dynamism.

As you arrive in Dar es Salaam, you are greeted by the sight of towering skyscrapers, bustling markets, and a colorful mix of people from various backgrounds. This cosmopolitan city is a melting pot of cultures, with influences from Arabic, Indian, African, and European traditions converging to create a unique and diverse urban tapestry.

Dar es Salaam's history dates back centuries, with its roots as a small fishing village along the East African coast. Over time, it evolved into a significant trading post and port, attracting merchants from Arabia, Persia, and India. The city's strategic location on the Indian Ocean made it a crucial center for the spice and slave trade, and its fortunes continued to grow with the arrival of European colonial powers in the 19th century.

Today, Dar es Salaam is a vibrant economic hub and Tanzania's largest city, with a population of over five million people. The city's economy is diverse, with sectors ranging from finance and commerce to manufacturing and tourism. It serves as the country's major port and gateway to international trade, connecting Tanzania to the global market.

The heart of Dar es Salaam is its bustling city center, where modern high-rises share space with historic buildings that hark back to the city's colonial past. The Azania Front Lutheran Church, a magnificent structure dating back to the late 19th century, stands as a prominent landmark, showcasing a blend of Gothic and Islamic architectural styles.

For a glimpse into Dar es Salaam's vibrant culture, head to the Kariakoo Market, a lively and bustling bazaar that offers a kaleidoscope of sights, sounds, and scents. Here, you can shop for fresh produce, spices, textiles, and traditional crafts, while immersing yourself in the energy and rhythm of everyday life in the city.

Dar es Salaam is also a city of green spaces and coastal beauty. The Coco Beach, located along the Indian Ocean, offers a relaxing escape from the urban bustle, with palm-fringed shores and inviting waters. Watching the sun dip below the horizon here is a cherished pastime for both locals and visitors alike.

One of Dar es Salaam's cultural gems is the National Museum of Tanzania, located in the city center. The museum houses a fascinating collection of artifacts, exhibits, and historical objects that showcase Tanzania's rich cultural heritage and natural history. It offers a window into the country's past, from its prehistoric origins to the struggles for independence and the journey to nationhood.

For those seeking to delve into the city's artistic scene, the Village Museum is a must-visit. This open-air museum offers a glimpse into the traditional lifestyles and cultures of Tanzania's various ethnic groups, with recreated traditional dwellings and exhibitions of traditional crafts and music.

As the sun sets, the city comes alive with a thriving nightlife scene. From lively bars and clubs to restaurants serving a diverse array of cuisines, Dar es Salaam offers plenty of options for those looking to unwind and enjoy the city's vibrant atmosphere.

Dar es Salaam's charm lies not only in its modern amenities and cosmopolitan character but also in the warmth and hospitality of its people. Tanzanians are known for their friendliness and welcoming nature, making visitors feel at home in this bustling urban center.

In this thriving metropolis, tradition and progress coexist, creating a city that embraces its past while moving forward with confidence and ambition. Dar es Salaam is a city of contrasts and diversity—a place where ancient traditions meet modern aspirations, and where the spirit of Tanzania's past is intricately woven into the fabric of its dynamic present.

Arusha: Gateway to Tanzania's Treasures

Nestled at the foothills of Mount Meru, Arusha is a charming city that serves as the gateway to some of Tanzania's most extraordinary treasures. This vibrant urban center, often referred to as the "Safari Capital of Tanzania," holds a special place in the hearts of travelers as they embark on their African adventures.

Arusha's strategic location makes it an ideal starting point for exploring Tanzania's renowned national parks and wildlife reserves. Within a short drive from the city lies the iconic Serengeti National Park, where the Great Migration—the world's largest mammal migration—takes place. This awe-inspiring spectacle sees millions of wildebeest and other herbivores journey across vast plains in search of fresh grazing lands.

For those seeking the thrill of a wildlife safari, Arusha is the gateway to the Ngorongoro Crater, a UNESCO World Heritage Site and a haven for diverse wildlife. This volcanic caldera is home to an array of animal species, including lions, elephants, buffalo, and the critically endangered black rhino.

The nearby Tarangire National Park is another treasure waiting to be explored. Famous for its large elephant herds and iconic baobab trees, Tarangire offers a unique safari experience with its picturesque landscapes and abundant wildlife.

Arusha is not just a paradise for safari enthusiasts—it also boasts a rich cultural scene and a fascinating history. The city is a melting pot of various ethnic groups, including the Maasai, Arusha, and Meru people, each contributing to the city's unique cultural tapestry.

A visit to the Arusha Cultural Heritage Centre is a window into Tanzania's diverse heritage, with its collection of traditional crafts, artwork, and artifacts. Here, visitors can learn about the country's history, traditions, and the unique way of life of its different ethnic groups.

The city's vibrant markets are a sensory delight, offering a chance to engage with local vendors and immerse oneself in the daily life of Arusha's residents. The Maasai Market, in particular, is a must-visit for those seeking authentic handcrafted souvenirs and the opportunity to interact with Maasai artisans.

Mount Meru, the city's iconic backdrop, offers adventurous travelers the opportunity to embark on a challenging trek to its summit. Often overshadowed by its famous neighbor, Mount Kilimanjaro, Mount Meru rewards climbers with breathtaking views and encounters with unique flora and fauna.

Arusha is also a hub for conservation and wildlife research. The city is home to several organizations dedicated to the preservation of Tanzania's natural wonders, including the African Wildlife Foundation and the Tanzanian Wildlife Research Institute.

Beyond its natural and cultural treasures, Arusha is a place of warmth and hospitality, where visitors are embraced by the friendly smiles of its inhabitants. The city's residents are known for their genuine warmth and welcoming nature, making travelers feel at home in this vibrant urban oasis.

Mwanza: Port City on the Shores of Lake Victoria

As you approach Mwanza, you'll be greeted by the breathtaking sight of Lake Victoria stretching out to the horizon, its sparkling waters reflecting the golden rays of the sun. Known as "The Rock City" due to the large rock formations that dot its landscape, Mwanza's scenery is a feast for the eyes, offering a unique blend of urban charm and natural beauty.

The city's strategic location as a port on Lake Victoria has made it a significant center for trade and commerce. As a major transportation hub, Mwanza connects Tanzania to neighboring countries, playing a crucial role in the movement of goods and people in the region.

The iconic Bismarck Rock, a massive granite outcrop that juts out into the lake, is one of Mwanza's most famous landmarks. It offers a stunning backdrop for photos and a vantage point to take in panoramic views of the lake and the city.

Mwanza's markets are a vibrant hub of activity, offering a kaleidoscope of sights, sounds, and smells. The bustling Soko Kuu Market, in the heart of the city, is a treasure trove of fresh produce, spices, and handcrafted goods. Here, you can immerse yourself in the local culture and witness the everyday hustle and bustle of Mwanza's residents.

Lake Victoria is not just a picturesque backdrop; it also provides ample opportunities for water-based activities. Fishing is a significant part of the local economy and a way of life for many who call Mwanza home. A boat ride on the lake offers a chance to witness the traditional fishing techniques and the timeless beauty of the surrounding landscape.

For those seeking adventure, the nearby Rubondo Island National Park is a hidden gem waiting to be discovered. This lush and untouched island sanctuary is home to diverse wildlife, including elephants, hippos, and chimpanzees. Exploring the island's untouched forests and pristine beaches is a unique experience that transports visitors to a world of untouched wilderness.

Mwanza is not just a place of natural beauty; it also boasts a rich cultural heritage. The city is home to various ethnic groups, including the Sukuma, the largest ethnic community in Tanzania. Engaging with the locals and learning about their customs and traditions is an enriching aspect of any visit to Mwanza.

The city's vibrant arts scene is another testament to its cultural richness. The Nyakato Art Market is a haven for local artists, showcasing a wide range of paintings, sculptures, and traditional crafts. Visitors can immerse themselves in the creative spirit of Mwanza and take home unique souvenirs that capture the essence of Tanzania's artistic talent.

As the sun sets over Lake Victoria, casting a warm glow over the city, Mwanza comes alive with its nightlife. Local restaurants and bars offer an opportunity to savor authentic Tanzanian cuisine, from grilled tilapia to delicious pilau rice, while enjoying the rhythmic beats of traditional music and dance.

Mwanza's charm lies not only in its natural beauty and cultural heritage but also in the warmth and hospitality of its people. The residents of Mwanza are known for their genuine friendliness, making visitors feel welcome and at home in this vibrant lakeside city.

Bagamoyo: A Historic Coastal Trading Post

Nestled along the azure waters of the Indian Ocean, Bagamoyo is a place where the past meets the present—a coastal town with a rich history that has left an indelible mark on Tanzania's identity. This historic trading post, whose name means "lay down your heart" in Swahili, has played a significant role in the region's cultural exchange and development over the centuries.

Bagamoyo's history dates back to the 18th century when it was established as a trading settlement by Arab traders from Oman. The town's strategic location along the East African coast made it a vital stop along the Indian Ocean trade routes, connecting merchants from Arabia, India, and the interior of Africa.

As a hub of commerce and cultural exchange, Bagamoyo attracted traders and explorers from various corners of the world. German explorer Carl Peters established a German East Africa Company office in Bagamoyo in the late 19th century, marking the beginning of German colonization in the region.

The town's historic significance is closely tied to its role in the East African slave trade. Bagamoyo was a major center for the slave trade, serving as a transit point where enslaved individuals were held before being shipped off to the markets in Zanzibar and beyond. The remnants of this dark chapter of history can be explored at the Bagamoyo Slave Market, a poignant reminder of the town's past.

Beyond its role in the slave trade, Bagamoyo played a pivotal role in the exploration of East Africa. Renowned British explorer David Livingstone began his famous journey to the interior of Africa from Bagamoyo in 1866. His explorations opened up new frontiers and paved the way for further expeditions into the heart of the continent.

Today, Bagamoyo is a town that pays homage to its history while embracing modernity. The town's architecture reflects a blend of Swahili, Arab, and European influences, with historic buildings and monuments scattered throughout its streets. The Catholic Church of Bagamoyo, a striking Gothic-style structure built in the late 19th century, stands as a testament to the town's colonial past.

The Bagamoyo Arts and Crafts Center is a thriving hub for local artists and artisans, where visitors can explore a diverse array of traditional crafts and artwork. The center offers a glimpse into the creativity and talent of the town's residents, who continue to carry on the legacy of craftsmanship passed down through generations.

Bagamoyo's coastal beauty is another highlight of the town. Its sandy shores and swaying palm trees invite visitors to bask in the serenity of the Indian Ocean. The town's proximity to Dar es Salaam, Tanzania's largest city, also makes it a popular weekend getaway for city dwellers seeking respite by the sea.

For those seeking a deeper understanding of Bagamoyo's past, the Bagamoyo Historical Tour offers a comprehensive exploration of the town's significant landmarks and sites. The tour takes visitors on a journey through time, with expert guides shedding light on the town's history and cultural heritage.

Bagamoyo's cultural significance extends beyond its borders. The town was designated a UNESCO World Heritage Site in 2006, recognizing its historical importance and the need for its preservation for future generations.

The charm of Bagamoyo lies not only in its historic significance but also in the warmth and hospitality of its people. The residents of Bagamoyo are known for their friendly nature and welcoming spirit, inviting visitors to experience the town's culture and traditions firsthand.

Cultural Diversity of Tanzania: A Melting Pot of Traditions

Step into the diverse and enchanting world of Tanzania—a land of rich cultural tapestry woven together by the traditions and customs of its people. The country's vibrant mosaic of ethnic groups, languages, and traditions make it a true melting pot of cultures, each contributing to the unique identity of Tanzania.

At the heart of Tanzania's cultural diversity are its numerous ethnic groups, each with its own distinct way of life and traditions. The largest ethnic group, the Sukuma, primarily resides in the northwestern region and is known for its strong agricultural practices and vibrant music and dance.

In the northern highlands, you'll find the Chagga people, renowned for their skilled farming and cultivation of coffee and bananas. The Chagga are also known for their elaborate traditional ceremonies, such as weddings and rites of passage.

Venture to the coastal regions, and you'll encounter the Swahili people, who have a deep-rooted history of trade and cultural exchange with the Arabian Peninsula and beyond. The Swahili language, a blend of Arabic and Bantu, is widely spoken throughout Tanzania and serves as a unifying linguistic thread that binds the nation together.

The Maasai people, with their distinctive clothing and intricate beadwork, are among the most recognizable ethnic groups in Tanzania. Renowned for their semi-nomadic lifestyle and strong attachment to their ancestral lands, the Maasai have preserved their traditional customs and cultural practices.

Tanzania's cultural diversity extends beyond its indigenous ethnic groups. The country is home to a significant population of Asian communities, particularly Indians, who have a long history of trade and settlement in Tanzania. This cultural fusion is evident in the cuisine and architecture of cities like Dar es Salaam, where traditional Indian spices and flavors intertwine with Swahili influences.

Religion also plays a vital role in Tanzania's cultural fabric. Islam is the dominant religion, with a large Muslim population concentrated in the coastal regions and on the island of Zanzibar. Christianity is practiced by a substantial portion of the population, particularly in the highlands and urban centers. The harmonious coexistence of different faiths exemplifies the nation's tolerance and respect for diverse religious beliefs.

One of the most cherished aspects of Tanzania's cultural heritage is its traditional music and dance. Each ethnic group has its own unique musical style and rhythm, reflecting the spirit and identity of their community. From the energetic rhythms of the ngoma drum dance to the melodious tunes of the kora, the music of Tanzania is a celebration of life and a reflection of its people's joys and sorrows.

Art and craftsmanship are also integral to Tanzania's cultural expression. The country's artisans create intricate wood carvings, colorful paintings, and finely woven textiles, showcasing their talents and preserving age-old techniques passed down through generations.

Traditional festivals and ceremonies offer a window into Tanzania's cultural vibrancy. Events like Makonde carving festivals and the Bagamoyo Arts Festival celebrate the country's artistic heritage and provide an opportunity for artists to showcase their talents.

Family and community bonds are highly valued in Tanzanian culture. Extended families often live together, and communal activities, such as farming and celebrating important milestones, strengthen the social fabric of the nation.

Despite its diverse cultural landscape, Tanzania takes pride in its national unity and identity. The Tanzanian flag, adorned with its black, yellow, and green colors, symbolizes the nation's unity and solidarity, while the national anthem sings praises to the nation's beauty and heritage.

Tanzania's cultural diversity is a source of strength and pride, enriching the nation's heritage and shaping its future. As you traverse the vast landscapes and interact with the warm-hearted people of Tanzania, you'll discover a country that cherishes its traditions while embracing progress and change.

The Maasai: Enduring Traditions and Modern Realities

The Maasai people of Tanzania embody a cultural heritage that has withstood the test of time—a captivating blend of tradition, resilience, and adaptation to the modern world. Known for their distinctive clothing, vibrant beadwork, and enduring attachment to their ancestral lands, the Maasai are a living testament to the rich cultural diversity that defines Tanzania.

The Maasai are a semi-nomadic ethnic group that primarily resides in the northern and central regions of Tanzania, as well as parts of Kenya. Renowned for their pastoral lifestyle, they have traditionally relied on cattle herding as a means of sustenance and livelihood. Their deep bond with cattle is reflected in their rituals, ceremonies, and folklore, making these majestic animals central to their way of life.

The Maasai are easily recognizable by their traditional clothing, which includes bright, colorful shukas (cloaks) draped over their shoulders and intricate beadwork adorning their necks, wrists, and ankles. The colors and patterns of their clothing hold significance and often represent different stages of life, achievements, and social status within the community.

Resilience is a defining characteristic of the Maasai people, who have adapted to various challenges throughout their history. From enduring conflicts with neighboring tribes to weathering the impacts of drought and changing landscapes, the Maasai have demonstrated remarkable adaptability to changing circumstances while preserving their core values and way of life.

However, like many indigenous communities, the Maasai face the realities of modernization and globalization. The encroachment of modern infrastructure, such as roads and settlements, has led to the fragmentation of their traditional grazing lands. The increasing demands of tourism have also placed pressures on their cultural practices and lands, leading to a delicate balancing act between preserving their heritage and participating in the modern economy.

Despite these challenges, the Maasai people continue to celebrate and share their cultural heritage with the world. Visitors to Maasai communities can witness the beauty of their traditional music and dance, which play a central role in their ceremonies and celebrations. The rhythmic chanting and mesmerizing movements evoke a sense of ancient wisdom and a deep connection to the land.

The Maasai are also known for their iconic jumping dance, a vibrant display of strength and agility performed during special occasions. This dance, known as "adumu" in the Maasai language, has captured the fascination of travelers and photographers, becoming a symbol of Maasai culture worldwide.

The community's social structure is organized around age sets, known as "age-sets" or "age-grades." Each age-set corresponds to a specific stage of life, and members of the same age-set share common experiences and responsibilities. Elders hold a revered position within the community, passing down traditional knowledge, wisdom, and customs to the younger generations.

Education is gradually becoming more accessible to Maasai children, providing opportunities for both formal education and the preservation of their cultural heritage. Efforts are being made to balance modern education with traditional teachings to ensure that Maasai youth retain their cultural identity while gaining the skills needed to navigate the modern world.

Cultural tourism initiatives have emerged as a means to support Maasai communities while fostering cultural exchange. Visitors to Maasai villages have the opportunity to learn about their customs, participate in traditional activities, and purchase authentic Maasai crafts, providing an avenue for economic empowerment while preserving their cultural practices.

The Maasai's resilience and determination to preserve their traditions in the face of modern realities serve as a testament to the enduring spirit of Tanzania's indigenous communities. Their cultural heritage is not just a relic of the past—it is a living, breathing testament to the resilience and adaptability of the human spirit.

The Hadza: Ancient Hunter-Gatherers of Tanzania

Deep within the rugged landscapes of Tanzania, the Hadza people stand as a living link to our ancient past—a resilient community of hunter-gatherers who have thrived in harmony with nature for thousands of years. As one of the last remaining hunter-gatherer tribes in East Africa, the Hadza offer a captivating glimpse into the way of life that once defined our shared human history.

The Hadza primarily reside in the Lake Eyasi region of northern Tanzania, where they have inhabited the land for over 10,000 years. Their traditional territory spans the acacia woodlands, savannas, and baobab-dotted landscapes, providing them with a diverse range of resources for sustenance and survival.

Hunter-gatherer societies, like the Hadza, have played a crucial role in shaping human evolution. Before the advent of agriculture and settled civilizations, our ancestors relied on hunting wild game and gathering fruits, tubers, and other plant resources to sustain themselves. The Hadza's lifestyle, rooted in this ancient way of life, offers invaluable insights into the practices and adaptability of early human communities.

The Hadza's hunting techniques are fascinating in their simplicity and effectiveness. Armed with bows and arrows, they venture into the bush, relying on their acute knowledge of the land and animal behavior to track and capture game. Their exceptional tracking skills, honed over generations, enable them to locate elusive animals with remarkable accuracy.

In addition to hunting, gathering plays a significant role in the Hadza's subsistence. Women are expert foragers, using their keen eyes and knowledge of seasonal patterns to locate edible plants, fruits, and honey from wild beehives. The Hadza's diet is incredibly diverse, featuring a variety of berries, nuts, tubers, and meat from the animals they hunt.

The Hadza's close relationship with nature is evident in their profound understanding of the environment. They possess an intricate knowledge of the medicinal properties of plants, using traditional herbal remedies to treat ailments and maintain their well-being.

Socially, the Hadza live in small, tight-knit bands, typically consisting of 20 to 30 individuals. Within the band, there is a sense of egalitarianism, as decisions are made collectively, and there is no centralized leadership. The community's cohesion and cooperation are essential for their survival in the challenging and unpredictable environment.

Despite the challenges posed by modernization and encroachment on their lands, the Hadza have managed to preserve their way of life. Their resilience in the face of change is a testament to their deep-rooted cultural identity and commitment to maintaining their hunter-gatherer traditions.

In recent years, the Hadza have increasingly faced external pressures that threaten their traditional way of life. Changes in land use and the establishment of wildlife reserves have restricted their access to hunting and gathering grounds, leading to concerns about their long-term survival and cultural preservation.

Efforts are being made by local and international organizations to support the Hadza in maintaining their cultural heritage and securing their land rights. Sustainable tourism initiatives have also emerged, offering visitors the opportunity to experience the Hadza's way of life and contribute to community-led conservation efforts.

The Hadza's existence as one of the last remaining hunter-gatherer communities reminds us of the vast diversity of human cultures that have shaped our shared history. Their story offers a poignant reflection on the resilience and adaptability of indigenous communities in the face of modern challenges.

Makonde: Masters of Wood Carvings

Deep within the heart of Tanzania, the Makonde people have carved a legacy of artistry that resonates across time and borders. Renowned for their exceptional wood carvings, the Makonde are true masters of their craft, producing intricate and captivating works of art that showcase their rich cultural heritage and artistic prowess.

The Makonde people are an ethnic group primarily residing in the southeastern regions of Tanzania, with a smaller population in northern Mozambique. They trace their roots back to the southeast of Africa, and their migration to Tanzania and Mozambique is believed to have taken place in the 18th and 19th centuries.

Wood carving is at the core of Makonde culture and identity, passed down through generations as a cherished tradition. The art of carving has been a means of storytelling, religious expression, and celebration within the community, capturing the essence of their lives, beliefs, and history.

The expertise of Makonde wood carvers is nothing short of awe-inspiring. Armed with simple tools like chisels, knives, and machetes, they transform blocks of hardwood, such as ebony, rosewood, and mpingo, into works of art that breathe with life and emotion. The attention to detail and the precision in their craftsmanship are a testament to the skill and dedication honed over decades of practice.

Makonde carvings often depict scenes from daily life, mythical creatures, ancestral spirits, and animals found in the region's rich biodiversity. Each piece tells a unique story, capturing the cultural identity and the connection between the Makonde people and their natural surroundings.

One of the most iconic and recognizable forms of Makonde carving is the Ujamaa family tree, representing the importance of family and community bonds. These intricate sculptures showcase a central human figure surrounded by a circle of smaller figures, symbolizing the unity and interconnectedness of the community.

Beyond their artistic significance, Makonde carvings hold cultural and spiritual importance for the community. Traditional rituals and ceremonies often feature carved masks and sculptures used in dance and religious practices. The carvings serve as a conduit for communication with ancestral spirits and play a vital role in preserving the community's cultural heritage.

The Makonde's artistic prowess has not gone unnoticed on the global stage. Their wood carvings have captured the attention of collectors, art enthusiasts, and tourists worldwide. Art galleries and exhibitions often feature Makonde sculptures, showcasing the depth and diversity of their artistic expressions.

The Makonde people have also faced challenges in preserving their craft and cultural heritage in the face of modernization. Changes in lifestyle, urbanization, and the allure of modern industries have impacted the continuity of traditional carving practices. Nevertheless, efforts are being made to support and promote Makonde artists, ensuring that their craft continues to thrive and evolve while maintaining its cultural authenticity.

In recent years, the government of Tanzania has recognized the cultural importance of Makonde wood carving and has taken steps to safeguard this art form. Art centers and cooperatives have been established to provide training, support, and market access to Makonde artists, empowering them to continue their craft while preserving their cultural heritage.

Visitors to Tanzania have the opportunity to witness the artistry of the Makonde people firsthand. Art markets, workshops, and cultural centers in regions like Dar es Salaam and Mtwara offer a glimpse into the world of Makonde wood carving, inviting travelers to immerse themselves in the beauty and creativity of this ancient art form.

Tinga Tinga Art: Vivid Colors and Stories

Tinga Tinga Art takes its name from the late Edward Saidi Tingatinga, a Tanzanian artist who pioneered this distinctive style in the 1960s. Born in the village of Namochelia in southern Tanzania, Tingatinga's artistic journey began when he decided to paint bicycle frames. His creativity soon extended to canvas, where he transformed ordinary scenes of wildlife and village life into extraordinary bursts of color and form.

At the core of Tinga Tinga Art lies a visual language that speaks of joy, humor, and the everyday experiences of Tanzanian life. The artists use a mix of acrylic paints and enamel, creating a mesmerizing effect of vibrant colors that dance across the canvas. Each brushstroke breathes life into the animals, birds, and people that populate the scenes, infusing them with a sense of whimsy and charm.

Tinga Tinga Art is renowned for its simplicity and storytelling nature. The artists depict the world around them in a stylized manner, with bold outlines and exaggerated features that give the paintings a distinctive flair. These paintings often feature African wildlife like elephants, lions, giraffes, and birds, as well as scenes of village life, folklore, and traditional ceremonies.

One of the defining characteristics of Tinga Tinga Art is the use of rich and vivid colors that evoke the vibrancy of the Tanzanian landscape. The artists draw inspiration from the lush greenery, golden savannas, and radiant sunsets that grace the country's natural beauty. These colors infuse the paintings with an unmistakable energy and playfulness, capturing the essence of life in Tanzania.

Beyond their visual appeal, Tinga Tinga paintings also serve as a form of oral tradition and cultural preservation. Many of the artworks depict traditional tales and folklore that have been passed down through generations. Each painting becomes a narrative that keeps the stories alive, ensuring that the cultural heritage and wisdom of Tanzania are celebrated and shared with the world.

Tinga Tinga Art has not only captured the hearts of Tanzanians but has also gained international recognition and acclaim. Today, Tinga Tinga paintings can be found in art galleries and private collections worldwide. The art form's popularity has led to the establishment of Tinga Tinga art markets and cooperatives, providing artists with opportunities to showcase their talent and sustain their livelihoods.

In recent years, Tinga Tinga Art has expanded beyond traditional paintings to encompass a wide range of artistic expressions, including sculptures, textiles, and decorative items. These diverse creations continue to celebrate the richness of Tanzanian culture and resonate with audiences around the globe.

As you delve into the world of Tinga Tinga Art, you are invited to immerse yourself in a symphony of colors and stories that speak of the beauty, humor, and spirit of Tanzania. Each stroke of the brush carries with it the echoes of the past, the laughter of the present, and the hopes of the future. The legacy of Tinga Tinga Art is a testament to the power of art in bridging cultures, inspiring imagination, and preserving the essence of a people and their land. So, embrace the journey into this captivating world of Tinga Tinga Art and let the vivid colors and stories transport you to the heart of Tanzania's artistic soul.

Music and Dance: A Rhythmic Tapestry of Tanzania

Tanzanian music is a vibrant mosaic of styles and influences that reflect the country's cultural diversity and historical connections. Traditional music, shaped by centuries of storytelling and ritual, coexists harmoniously with modern genres, such as hip hop, reggae, and bongo flava. Each genre carries with it a unique narrative, celebrating the joys and struggles of Tanzanian life.

In the rural communities, traditional music remains deeply rooted in the daily lives of the people. The rhythmic sounds of drums, rattles, and xylophones echo across the plains as villagers come together to celebrate weddings, harvests, and rites of passage. These music gatherings foster a sense of community and belonging, connecting people to their cultural heritage and the spirit of their ancestors.

One of Tanzania's most celebrated musical traditions is Taarab, an elegant and melodious genre that originated in Zanzibar during the 19th century. Taarab music combines Arabic, Indian, and African influences, creating a unique blend of cultures and sounds. It is often accompanied by a full ensemble of instruments, including violins, ouds, qanuns, and percussion, and its poetic lyrics explore themes of love, longing, and the complexities of human emotions.

In contrast, the lively beats of Bongo Flava, a contemporary genre, resonate through the urban centers of Tanzania. Emerging in the 1990s, Bongo Flava incorporates elements of hip hop, R&B, and dancehall, blending global influences with local Swahili lyrics. Bongo Flava artists address social issues, politics, and matters of the heart, making it a powerful form of expression for Tanzanian youth.

Dance is an inseparable companion to Tanzanian music, providing a captivating visual representation of the music's soul. Each region of Tanzania boasts its own unique dance traditions, from the rhythmic hip-swaying of the Makonde people to the acrobatic leaps of the Maasai warriors. Dance is an integral part of cultural celebrations, storytelling, and spiritual rituals, allowing the dancers to embody the essence of their heritage.

The Gogo tribe, for instance, showcases the energetic and rhythmic Mganda dance, performed during various ceremonies to invoke the spirits and seek blessings. The Chagga people of Kilimanjaro region perform the lively Kidumbak dance, accompanied by the melodious sounds of the marimba, celebrating the joys of life and love.

In the coastal regions, the Taarab-inspired dances called "lelele" and "mduara" infuse celebrations with elegance and grace. These dances often involve intricate hand movements, graceful steps, and vibrant costumes, transporting the audience into a world of timeless beauty and sophistication.

Tanzanian music and dance have not only shaped the country's cultural identity but have also gained recognition on the global stage. Artists like Bi Kidude, Saida Karoli, and Diamond Platnumz have achieved international acclaim, introducing the world to the rich musical heritage of Tanzania.

The government of Tanzania has played a pivotal role in supporting and preserving the country's musical traditions. National cultural festivals and events, such as the Bagamoyo Festival of Arts and Culture, provide platforms for artists to showcase their talents and celebrate the nation's diverse artistic expressions.

Visitors to Tanzania have the opportunity to immerse themselves in the vibrant world of music and dance, experiencing the rhythmic pulse that defines the nation's soul. Cultural tourism initiatives offer travelers a chance to witness traditional performances, participate in dance workshops, and engage with local musicians, fostering a deep appreciation for Tanzania's artistic treasures.

The Swahili Language: Heartbeat of the Nation

In the heart of Tanzania, a rhythmic cadence reverberates through the air—the captivating melody of the Swahili language, an essential thread that weaves together the diverse tapestry of the nation. As the official language of Tanzania, Swahili serves as a unifying force, uniting people from different ethnic backgrounds and regions in a harmonious symphony of communication and culture.

Swahili, also known as Kiswahili, is a Bantu language with a rich history that stretches back centuries. It emerged as a lingua franca along the East African coast, where Arabic traders, Indian merchants, and African communities interacted for centuries in a bustling network of commerce and cultural exchange. Over time, Swahili absorbed influences from Arabic, Persian, Portuguese, and other African languages, evolving into the elegant and expressive language we know today.

One of the defining features of Swahili is its simplicity and ease of learning. With a straightforward phonetic system and a lack of complex verb conjugations, Swahili is accessible to both native speakers and foreign learners. This linguistic accessibility has contributed to its widespread adoption and use as a second language in many countries across East Africa.

In 1967, the Tanzanian government declared Swahili as the official language of the nation, recognizing its potential to promote national unity and cultural identity. Today, Swahili is spoken by the majority of Tanzanians, serving as a means of communication in schools, government institutions, media, and daily interactions.

Beyond its role as a lingua franca, Swahili plays a crucial role in preserving Tanzanian culture and heritage. The language is a repository of traditional stories, proverbs, and oral histories, passed down through generations. Swahili poetry, known as "ushairi," is a cherished art form that captures the spirit of Tanzanian life through eloquent verses and metaphors.

Swahili's cultural significance extends beyond Tanzania's borders. It serves as the official language in Kenya, Uganda, Rwanda, and the Democratic Republic of Congo. As a result, Swahili connects over 100 million people in East Africa, fostering regional cooperation and understanding.

In recent years, the popularity of Swahili has grown internationally, thanks to its portrayal in movies, music, and literature. Swahili phrases and expressions have found their way into popular culture, enriching the global linguistic landscape and contributing to a sense of cross-cultural appreciation.

The Tanzanian government has taken significant steps to promote Swahili on the international stage. The language is taught in schools and universities worldwide, fostering cultural exchange and enhancing diplomatic relations. International organizations, such as the African Union and the East African Community, have recognized Swahili as a key language for regional integration and communication.

In the vibrant streets of Dar es Salaam and the bustling markets of Zanzibar, Swahili echoes through conversations, music, and laughter—a living testament to its enduring role as the heartbeat of the nation. It is a language of warmth and hospitality, connecting people in shared experiences, whether they are strangers meeting for the first time or old friends reuniting after years apart.

As you immerse yourself in the magic of Tanzania, let the sweet melodies of Swahili wash over you, inviting you to join in the celebration of language and culture. Embrace the spirit of "karibu," which means "welcome" in Swahili, as you embark on a journey of discovery and connection, guided by the heartbeat of the nation—Swahili, a language that unites, inspires, and resonates in the hearts of millions.

Traditional Festivals and Celebrations

Tanzania comes alive with a vibrant tapestry of traditional festivals and celebrations, each one a joyful expression of the nation's cultural richness and diversity. Throughout the year, communities across Tanzania gather to honor ancient traditions, celebrate life's milestones, and pay homage to their ancestors.

One of the most significant festivals in Tanzania is the Swahili New Year, known as "Mwaka Kogwa" in Zanzibar and "Nyerere Day" on the mainland. This festival, celebrated in mid-July, marks the beginning of the Islamic calendar and serves as a time for purification and renewal. People gather to engage in traditional rituals, including the symbolic beating of banana stems, representing the release of negativity and the embrace of positivity for the year ahead.

Another cherished celebration is "Eid al-Fitr," the festival that marks the end of Ramadan, the Islamic holy month of fasting. Tanzanian Muslims come together to pray, exchange greetings, and share festive meals with family and friends. This joyous occasion fosters a spirit of unity and generosity, as communities extend a helping hand to those in need through charitable acts and donations.

In the coastal regions of Tanzania, "Sauti za Busara" takes center stage—a vibrant music festival that showcases the best of East African music and culture. Held annually in Stone Town, Zanzibar, the festival attracts music enthusiasts from around the world. It serves as a platform for both established and upcoming artists to celebrate the richness of African rhythms and melodies.

As the harvest season approaches, Tanzanian communities come together to celebrate "Nane Nane" (meaning "eight eight" in Swahili), also known as Farmer's Day. This agricultural fair takes place on August 8th and is a time for farmers to showcase their produce, livestock, and agricultural innovations. It also provides a platform for the exchange of knowledge and expertise, fostering advancements in farming practices.

The "Mkutano wa Chama Cha Mapinduzi" (CCM National Congress) is a significant political event that occurs every five years. During this congress, the ruling political party, CCM, gathers to discuss policy matters, elect leaders, and set the party's agenda for the future. It is a time of political engagement and reflection on the nation's progress and challenges.

"Tanzania Independence Day" on December 9th commemorates the country's liberation from colonial rule. Tanzanians come together to honor the sacrifices of their freedom fighters and celebrate the nation's sovereignty and unity. Festivities include parades, cultural performances, and patriotic displays that evoke a sense of national pride.

The "Bagamoyo Festival of Arts and Culture" is a week-long celebration of artistic expression and cultural heritage. Held annually in the coastal town of Bagamoyo, the festival brings together artists, musicians, dancers, and storytellers from across Tanzania and beyond. It is a time for creativity to flourish, cultural exchange to thrive, and the beauty of Tanzanian traditions to shine.

In the heart of Serengeti National Park, the "Wildebeest Migration" unfolds—an awe-inspiring natural spectacle that captivates both locals and visitors alike. This annual migration, where millions of wildebeests and other animals traverse the plains in search of greener pastures, is a symbol of the circle of life and the resilience of the natural world.

The "Kilimanjaro Marathon" is a thrilling sporting event that draws runners from around the globe to challenge themselves against the backdrop of Africa's tallest peak. Held annually, this marathon showcases the spirit of determination and adventure that defines Tanzania's mountaineering culture.

Spirituality and Religion in Tanzanian Society

In the vibrant tapestry of Tanzanian society, spirituality and religion form a cornerstone, interwoven into the fabric of daily life and cultural practices. As a diverse nation with over 120 ethnic groups, Tanzania boasts a wide array of religious beliefs and practices, creating a colorful mosaic of faith that reflects the country's historical connections and cultural heritage.

Religion in Tanzania is as varied as its landscapes, encompassing Christianity, Islam, traditional African religions, and a small Hindu and Sikh community. Each religion has its own traditions, rituals, and places of worship, contributing to the nation's religious pluralism and tolerance.

Christianity arrived in Tanzania through the efforts of European missionaries during the 19th century. Today, it is the largest religion in the country, with adherents from various denominations, including Roman Catholicism, Protestantism, and Anglicanism. The church plays an essential role in Tanzanian society, providing not only spiritual guidance but also educational and healthcare services to the community.

Islam holds a significant presence in Tanzania, particularly along the coast and in Zanzibar. Arab traders and settlers brought Islam to the region centuries ago, and it has since become deeply rooted in the cultural fabric of the Swahili-speaking communities. Mosques and Islamic schools dot the landscape, serving as centers of worship and education.

Alongside organized religions, traditional African religions remain a vital part of Tanzania's spiritual landscape. These beliefs are deeply intertwined with nature and ancestral worship, honoring the spirits of the land, water, and sky. Ceremonies and rituals are held to seek blessings, protection, and guidance from ancestors and spiritual beings.

The diversity of religious beliefs in Tanzania fosters a spirit of interfaith harmony and coexistence. Tanzanians often celebrate religious holidays together, irrespective of their faith. For instance, during Christmas and Eid, Christians and Muslims join in festive celebrations, exchanging greetings and gifts.

Tanzanian society is characterized by a sense of spiritual interconnectedness with nature. This reverence for the environment is evident in rituals and ceremonies held to honor rain, harvest, and other natural phenomena. Respect for nature and conservation efforts are deeply ingrained in the cultural consciousness of Tanzanians.

The role of spirituality goes beyond religious observance; it permeates every aspect of Tanzanian life. From birth to death, religious and spiritual rituals mark significant milestones. Naming ceremonies, marriage rites, and funeral traditions reflect the religious and cultural identity of the individuals and their communities.

The Tanzanian government upholds freedom of religion, enshrining it in the country's constitution. This commitment to religious freedom has contributed to the nation's harmonious coexistence among diverse faith communities. Interfaith dialogues and collaborations are encouraged, fostering mutual understanding and respect.

Tanzania is also a pilgrimage destination for followers of different faiths. The holy city of Bagamoyo holds significance for both Christians and Muslims, as it served as a historic center for missionary activities and the slave trade. Zanzibar attracts visitors seeking spiritual solace and enlightenment, drawn by its historical connections to Islam.

Spirituality and religion in Tanzania are not confined to places of worship; they extend into art, music, and dance. Traditional music and dance play a vital role in religious celebrations, reflecting the joy and reverence of the community's faith.

In the rural areas, spiritual healers and diviners, known as "mgangas," are respected members of the community. They use herbs, incantations, and rituals to provide healing and guidance to those seeking spiritual or physical assistance.

Education and Literacy: Nurturing Tomorrow's Leaders

In the quest for progress and development, Tanzania places a strong emphasis on education and literacy as the bedrock for nurturing tomorrow's leaders. The nation recognizes that investing in its youth and providing them with quality education is essential for fostering a skilled workforce, promoting social cohesion, and achieving sustainable growth.

The Tanzanian education system is structured into three levels: primary education, secondary education, and higher education. Primary education is free and compulsory for all children between the ages of 7 and 15. The government has made significant efforts to increase primary school enrollment rates and reduce disparities in access to education across regions.

Efforts to improve literacy rates in Tanzania have yielded positive results. According to UNICEF, the literacy rate among youth (aged 15-24) reached 76% in recent years, a testament to the nation's commitment to expanding educational opportunities. However, challenges remain in addressing gender disparities and ensuring access to quality education for marginalized groups.

In rural areas, where infrastructure and resources are limited, community involvement plays a crucial role in supporting educational initiatives. Local leaders, parents, and teachers work together to create conducive learning environments and encourage student retention.

To enhance the quality of education, the Tanzanian government has implemented various reforms, including teacher training programs, curriculum updates, and the integration of technology in classrooms. These efforts aim to equip teachers with the necessary skills and knowledge to deliver effective and innovative instruction.

Secondary education in Tanzania is not yet fully free, leading to some dropouts due to financial constraints. Nevertheless, the government is working to make secondary education more accessible and affordable for all Tanzanian youth.

Technical and vocational education and training (TVET) programs have gained prominence in Tanzania, as they provide practical skills and knowledge that align with the demands of the job market. These programs empower students to enter the workforce with marketable skills, contributing to economic growth and reducing unemployment rates.

Beyond formal education, non-governmental organizations (NGOs) and community-based initiatives play a vital role in promoting literacy and education. These organizations work to establish libraries, provide scholarships, and offer educational support to marginalized groups, fostering inclusivity and empowering Tanzanian youth to reach their full potential.

Tanzania's higher education system is expanding, with universities and colleges offering diverse academic programs. The government is committed to fostering research and innovation in higher education to address the country's development challenges and harness the potential of its young scholars.

As technology continues to evolve, e-learning and online education platforms are gaining popularity in Tanzania. These platforms offer a flexible and accessible approach to learning, enabling students in remote areas to access educational resources and connect with educators.

In recent years, Tanzania has made significant progress in promoting girl's education, recognizing the importance of gender equality in education. Initiatives such as the "Elimu kwa Mnyonge" (Education for the Vulnerable) program aim to address the barriers faced by girls in accessing education and improving their academic outcomes.

As Tanzania continues to invest in education and literacy, it paves the way for a brighter future, where empowered and educated young leaders will drive the nation forward. Education is a powerful tool for social transformation, fostering critical thinking, creativity, and empathy—essential qualities for tomorrow's leaders as they navigate the complexities of a rapidly changing world.

Healthcare and Challenges in Tanzania

In Tanzania, the pursuit of good health and well-being is an ongoing journey, shaped by a complex landscape of opportunities and challenges. As a nation committed to improving healthcare for its citizens, Tanzania grapples with a range of issues, from limited resources to disparities in access to medical services.

Healthcare in Tanzania is a critical priority for the government, as evidenced by its commitment to achieving the United Nations Sustainable Development Goals (SDGs), particularly Goal 3: Good Health and Well-being. Efforts to improve healthcare have led to progress in various areas, but challenges persist.

One of the most significant challenges is the shortage of healthcare facilities, particularly in rural and remote areas. Many communities lack access to primary healthcare centers, leading to long distances that people must travel to seek medical attention. This issue disproportionately affects vulnerable populations, including women, children, and the elderly.

Inadequate infrastructure and medical equipment pose further obstacles to the delivery of quality healthcare services. Some healthcare facilities lack essential medical equipment, leading to difficulties in diagnosing and treating patients effectively. The shortage of medical personnel, including doctors, nurses, and other healthcare professionals, also impacts the overall quality of care.

The burden of communicable diseases, such as malaria, HIV/AIDS, and tuberculosis, remains a significant challenge for Tanzania's healthcare system. While efforts have been made to combat these diseases, there is a need for continued investment in prevention, treatment, and awareness programs to further reduce their impact.

Maternal and child health is another critical area of concern. Despite progress in reducing maternal and infant mortality rates, Tanzania still faces challenges in providing adequate maternal care and access to skilled birth attendants. Additionally, malnutrition remains a concern for child health and development.

Tanzania's healthcare system also faces challenges related to non-communicable diseases (NCDs), including cardiovascular diseases, diabetes, and cancer. As lifestyles change and urbanization increases, the prevalence of NCDs is on the rise. Addressing this issue requires a comprehensive approach, including prevention, early detection, and access to treatment.

The cost of healthcare can be a significant barrier for many Tanzanians, especially those living in poverty. While efforts have been made to provide free or subsidized healthcare services, the financial burden of medical expenses remains a challenge for some individuals and families.

To improve healthcare access and delivery, the Tanzanian government has implemented various initiatives. These include the establishment of the National Health Insurance Fund (NHIF), which aims to provide affordable health coverage to a broader segment of the population. The government has also increased investments in healthcare infrastructure and human resources.

In recent years, the COVID-19 pandemic has presented additional challenges to Tanzania's healthcare system. The government has taken measures to combat the spread of the virus, but there have been debates over data transparency and reporting. Like many countries worldwide, Tanzania has faced the need to balance public health measures with economic and social considerations.

Despite these challenges, there is a sense of resilience and determination among Tanzanian healthcare professionals and communities. NGOs and international organizations also play a crucial role in supporting healthcare initiatives in Tanzania, working in partnership with the government to address health disparities and improve outcomes.

The Tanzanian Economy: Past and Present

The Tanzanian economy has undergone significant transformations over the years, shaping its past and influencing its present. As a country rich in natural resources and diverse economic potential, Tanzania has strived to navigate various challenges and opportunities on its journey towards economic growth and development.

In the early post-independence era, Tanzania pursued a socialist economic model under the leadership of Julius Nyerere, known as "Ujamaa." The focus was on collective ownership of land and resources, with the goal of reducing income disparities and promoting communal development. During this period, agriculture played a central role in the economy, providing livelihoods for the majority of the population.

In the 1980s, Tanzania faced economic hardships, resulting from a combination of internal and external factors. External debt burdens, declining commodity prices, and unfavorable international trade conditions contributed to a challenging economic environment. In response, the Tanzanian government embarked on economic reforms, including liberalization and structural adjustment policies.

The 1990s marked a significant turning point for Tanzania's economy. The country shifted from a centralized, state-controlled economy to a more market-oriented approach. This move towards economic liberalization aimed to attract foreign investment, boost private sector growth, and diversify the economy beyond agriculture.

Tanzania's economic growth gained momentum in the early 2000s, supported by favorable macroeconomic policies and increased investments in infrastructure and human capital. The discovery of natural gas reserves off the coast of Tanzania in 2010 further enhanced the country's economic prospects, opening new opportunities in the energy sector.

Today, Tanzania boasts one of the fastest-growing economies in Africa. Its GDP has been steadily increasing, driven by sectors such as agriculture, mining, manufacturing, and services. Agriculture remains a significant contributor to the economy, employing the majority of the population and supplying vital export commodities such as coffee, tea, and cashew nuts.

The mining sector has also emerged as a critical component of Tanzania's economy, with the country being a major producer of gold and other minerals. Foreign investment in mining projects has surged, contributing to export earnings and government revenue.

Tourism has become an essential pillar of the Tanzanian economy, attracting travelers from around the globe with its rich natural beauty and wildlife. From the vast savannahs of the Serengeti to the exotic beaches of Zanzibar, Tanzania offers a diverse range of attractions that contribute significantly to the country's foreign exchange earnings.

The services sector, including finance, telecommunications, and trade, has experienced rapid growth, reflecting increased urbanization and a burgeoning middle class. Tanzanians' access to mobile banking services has expanded, contributing to financial inclusion and economic empowerment.

Despite these positive developments, Tanzania still faces challenges in achieving inclusive and sustainable economic growth. Income inequality remains a concern, with disparities between urban and rural areas, as well as different regions of the country. Addressing these disparities requires targeted policies and investments to ensure that economic opportunities are accessible to all.

The Tanzanian government continues to implement economic reforms to attract foreign investment, promote private sector development, and enhance the business environment. Improving infrastructure, including roads, ports, and energy supply, is a priority to support economic activities and regional integration.

The country's young and growing population presents both opportunities and challenges for the economy. With a sizable youth labor force, investing in education, skills development, and job creation is crucial to harness the demographic dividend and drive economic productivity.

Mining and Natural Resources: Blessing or Curse?

Mining and natural resources in Tanzania have long been a subject of both excitement and controversy. On one hand, these valuable assets offer immense potential for economic growth, job creation, and foreign investment. On the other hand, the extraction and management of these resources come with complex challenges, including environmental concerns and the risk of resource depletion.

Tanzania is rich in diverse natural resources, including minerals, precious metals, natural gas, and vast arable land. The country's mining sector has been a significant contributor to its economy, particularly with the discovery of substantial gold reserves and other minerals. Mining activities have attracted foreign investors, creating employment opportunities and generating government revenue through taxes and royalties.

The gold mining industry in Tanzania has experienced remarkable growth, with the country being one of Africa's leading gold producers. Geita Gold Mine and Bulyanhulu Gold Mine are among the notable gold mines that have contributed to Tanzania's economic prosperity. Additionally, the mining sector has expanded to include the extraction of gemstones, such as tanzanite, which is unique to the country.

The discovery of natural gas reserves off the coast of Tanzania has added a new dimension to the country's natural resource wealth. These reserves present significant potential for energy production and export, providing an opportunity for Tanzania to become a regional energy hub. Natural gas has become a critical component of Tanzania's energy mix, reducing reliance on costly imported fossil fuels.

However, the mining and extraction of natural resources have not been without challenges. Environmental concerns related to mining practices, such as deforestation, water pollution, and habitat destruction, have raised alarm bells among environmentalists and local communities. Balancing economic development with sustainable environmental practices remains an ongoing challenge.

Another issue of concern is the impact of mining on communities living near mining sites. The relocation of communities to make way for mining operations has sometimes led to social tensions and disputes over land rights. Local communities may also feel excluded from the benefits of mining activities, leading to grievances and calls for equitable distribution of resources.

Transparency and governance in the mining sector have been areas of scrutiny. Ensuring that the revenue generated from mining activities benefits the country as a whole, rather than being subject to corruption or mismanagement, is a crucial aspect of resource governance. Efforts to enhance transparency and accountability in the sector are essential to ensuring that mining benefits the nation's development.

Furthermore, the volatility of commodity prices can have significant effects on Tanzania's economy, as witnessed during periods of global economic fluctuations. Overreliance on a particular resource can expose the country to external market risks, necessitating diversification of the economy.

Addressing the challenges associated with mining and natural resources requires a comprehensive approach. The Tanzanian government has made efforts to enhance the regulatory framework for the mining sector, promoting responsible mining practices and environmental protection. The implementation of the Extractive Industries Transparency Initiative (EITI) has aimed to increase transparency and public participation in resource management. Additionally, local content policies have been introduced to ensure that Tanzanian companies and communities benefit from mining operations through procurement and employment opportunities.

Conservation and Environmental Issues

Conservation and environmental issues are at the forefront of Tanzania's efforts to safeguard its unique natural heritage for future generations. With its diverse ecosystems, abundant wildlife, and stunning landscapes, Tanzania is a treasure trove of biodiversity and ecological wonders.

One of the most iconic conservation areas in Tanzania is the Serengeti National Park. Known for its annual wildebeest migration, the park is a symbol of Africa's untamed wilderness. It provides a safe haven for a myriad of wildlife species, including the "Big Five" (elephant, lion, buffalo, leopard, and rhinoceros), cheetahs, giraffes, and numerous bird species.

Conservation efforts in Tanzania are not limited to national parks; the country has established a network of protected areas, including game reserves, marine parks, and forest reserves. These protected areas are essential for preserving biodiversity and promoting ecological balance.

Tanzania is also home to Mount Kilimanjaro, Africa's tallest peak. As a UNESCO World Heritage Site, Kilimanjaro faces the challenges of climate change and its impact on the fragile mountain ecosystems. The retreating glaciers on Kilimanjaro are a stark reminder of the urgent need to address global environmental issues.

Deforestation is a significant concern in Tanzania, driven by various factors such as logging, charcoal production, and land conversion for agriculture. This loss of forest cover poses threats to wildlife habitats, water resources, and climate stability. The government and environmental organizations are working together to combat deforestation through reforestation and sustainable land management practices.

Illegal wildlife poaching remains a pressing issue, particularly for species like elephants and rhinos, which are targeted for their ivory and horns. The demand for these products in international markets fuels poaching activities, despite the strict enforcement measures put in place by Tanzanian authorities.

To combat wildlife trafficking, Tanzania collaborates with global initiatives to curb the illegal wildlife trade. The country also engages in anti-poaching patrols and community-based conservation efforts to protect its wildlife treasures.

Another environmental challenge in Tanzania is water scarcity and pollution. Rapid urbanization and industrial activities contribute to the pollution of water bodies, affecting both human health and aquatic ecosystems. Sustainable water management practices and wastewater treatment are essential to ensure the availability of clean and safe water resources.

Climate change poses significant threats to Tanzania's environment and communities. The country is vulnerable to extreme weather events, including droughts, floods, and coastal erosion. These impacts have implications for agriculture, food security, and livelihoods, particularly for rural communities that depend on rain-fed agriculture.

Tanzania is taking steps to adapt to climate change and reduce greenhouse gas emissions. The country is investing in renewable energy projects, such as solar and wind power, to transition towards a more sustainable energy mix. Additionally, climate resilience initiatives aim to support vulnerable communities in adapting to changing environmental conditions.

Community-based conservation initiatives are instrumental in promoting conservation and sustainable resource management. Engaging local communities in conservation efforts empowers them to become stewards of their natural environment, fostering a sense of ownership and responsibility.

Women Empowerment and Gender Equality

In recent years, Tanzania has made significant strides in promoting women's empowerment and gender equality. Historically, like many other societies, Tanzanian women faced gender disparities and limitations on their opportunities. However, the country's commitment to advancing gender equality has led to transformative changes and improved prospects for women across various spheres of life.

Education is a critical pillar of women's empowerment in Tanzania. The government has implemented policies to ensure equal access to education for girls and boys. Efforts to reduce gender disparities in school enrollment and retention have yielded positive results, with more girls now accessing primary and secondary education.

Moreover, initiatives such as school feeding programs and incentives for families to send their daughters to school have helped increase attendance rates. Education empowers girls by equipping them with knowledge and skills, enhancing their employability, and enabling them to make informed decisions about their lives.

In the realm of politics and leadership, Tanzania has seen progress in enhancing women's participation and representation. Quota systems have been introduced to increase women's representation in parliament and local government. As a result, more women have been elected to public office, enabling them to actively contribute to policymaking and governance.

Women's economic empowerment has also been a focal point of efforts to achieve gender equality. Tanzania recognizes that empowering women economically benefits society as a whole. The country has implemented various programs to support women entrepreneurs, provide access to credit and financial services, and promote women's participation in the formal labor market.

In agriculture, which is a vital sector of Tanzania's economy, women play a crucial role as small-scale farmers and food producers. Recognizing the significance of their contributions, initiatives have been launched to enhance women's access to agricultural resources, including land, seeds, and technology. By empowering women farmers, Tanzania seeks to improve food security and rural livelihoods.

The fight against gender-based violence (GBV) has been a priority for the Tanzanian government and civil society organizations. Efforts to combat GBV include legal reforms, public awareness campaigns, and the establishment of support services for survivors. Despite these efforts, challenges remain in addressing deeply ingrained cultural norms and attitudes that perpetuate violence against women.

In rural communities, traditional practices such as female genital mutilation (FGM) have been a focus of efforts to protect women and girls from harm. Education and advocacy campaigns have led to a decline in the prevalence of FGM, though it still persists in some areas.

Women's access to healthcare, including reproductive health services, is another aspect of gender equality in Tanzania. Initiatives to improve maternal and child health have been instrumental in reducing maternal mortality rates and improving maternal health outcomes. Access to family planning services is vital to empowering women to make decisions about their reproductive health and overall well-being.

Non-governmental organizations (NGOs) and international partners have been instrumental in supporting women's empowerment initiatives in Tanzania. Their collaborative efforts with the government have helped mobilize resources and expertise to advance gender equality and uplift women's status in society.

Sports and Recreation: Passion for Football and Beyond

Sports and recreation hold a special place in the hearts of Tanzanians, with football being the most beloved and widely followed sport in the country. From the bustling streets to the serene rural villages, football brings people together, transcending age, gender, and social status. The passion for the sport is evident in the enthusiasm and energy displayed by fans during matches and the vibrant atmosphere in stadiums across the nation.

Tanzania has a rich football history, with the sport introduced by colonial powers in the early 20th century. Over the years, football has become deeply ingrained in the country's culture, with local teams and leagues flourishing in cities and towns. The Tanzanian Premier League attracts devoted fans who rally behind their favorite teams with unwavering loyalty.

The national football team, known as the Taifa Stars, represents Tanzania in international competitions. While they have not achieved significant success on the global stage, their participation in regional and continental tournaments, such as the Africa Cup of Nations (AFCON), fills Tanzanians with pride and a sense of national identity.

Beyond football, Tanzania boasts a diverse range of sports and recreational activities that cater to various interests and talents. Athletics, particularly long-distance running, has gained popularity, with Tanzanian athletes showcasing their prowess in marathons and road races worldwide. The success of Tanzanian runners like Filbert Bayi and Juma Ikangaa has inspired aspiring athletes across the country.

Basketball, volleyball, netball, and cricket are also enjoyed by many, especially in schools and local communities. These sports provide opportunities for young talents to hone their skills and compete in national and international events.

Tanzania's stunning landscapes and natural wonders offer the perfect backdrop for outdoor and adventure sports. Mountaineering enthusiasts from around the world flock to climb Mount Kilimanjaro, seeking the exhilarating experience of conquering Africa's highest peak. Mount Meru, another prominent mountain in Tanzania, also attracts trekkers and adventurers.

Water sports enthusiasts can indulge in diving, snorkeling, and swimming along the picturesque coastline of the Indian Ocean and the turquoise waters of Zanzibar. Tanzania's vast lakes, such as Lake Victoria and Lake Tanganyika, offer opportunities for boating, fishing, and water-based recreation.

Conservation areas and national parks in Tanzania present unique opportunities for wildlife enthusiasts and nature lovers. Safari tours provide a chance to witness the incredible diversity of wildlife, including lions, elephants, giraffes, and wildebeests, in their natural habitats. Serengeti National Park and the Ngorongoro Crater are among the most sought-after destinations for safari experiences.

Tanzania also participates in various regional and international sports events, fostering camaraderie and competition with neighboring countries and beyond. These events contribute to strengthening regional ties and promoting Tanzanian talent on the global stage.

Moreover, sports development and promotion receive support from the Tanzanian government and sports governing bodies. Investments in sports infrastructure, training facilities, and coaching programs aim to nurture a new generation of athletes and raise the country's profile in the sporting arena.

Nurturing the Tanzanian Arts and Literature

In the heart of East Africa lies Tanzania, a nation teeming with vibrant artistic expressions and a rich literary heritage. The arts and literature play a significant role in shaping the cultural identity of the Tanzanian people, celebrating their diversity and preserving their stories for generations to come.

Tanzania's artistic traditions are as diverse as its landscapes, with each region contributing unique flavors to the country's creative tapestry. Traditional dance and music are deeply rooted in Tanzanian culture, with rhythmic beats and colorful movements reflecting the customs and beliefs of various ethnic groups.

The Makonde people, renowned for their intricate wood carvings, produce stunning sculptures that narrate tales of their ancestral heritage. Tinga Tinga art, characterized by vivid colors and whimsical storytelling, captures the essence of wildlife and everyday life in Tanzania. These forms of visual art have gained international recognition and become sources of pride for Tanzanian artists and art enthusiasts alike.

Contemporary Tanzanian artists continue to explore new avenues of expression, blending traditional techniques with modern mediums. The country's art scene is alive with galleries, exhibitions, and art festivals that showcase the diverse talents of local artists and provide opportunities for them to engage with a global audience.

Literature has also played a crucial role in Tanzania's cultural development, with a rich tradition of storytelling passed down through generations. Oral literature, such as folktales and myths, has been a means of passing down history, wisdom, and moral values from one generation to another.

In the 20th century, Tanzanian writers began to emerge, expressing their experiences and perspectives through written words. Renowned authors like Shaaban Robert and Gabriel Ruhumbika used Swahili, the national language, to tell stories that resonated with Tanzanians across the country.

Tanzania's literary landscape has grown over the years, with writers exploring a range of themes, from social issues and political commentary to personal reflections on identity and belonging. The country's literature encompasses a diverse range of genres, including novels, short stories, poetry, and plays.

The government of Tanzania recognizes the importance of nurturing the arts and literature and has been supportive of initiatives that promote cultural expression and creativity. Funding for arts programs, literary festivals, and workshops provide a platform for artists and writers to hone their skills and share their work with the public.

Moreover, educational institutions play a significant role in fostering artistic talents and promoting literary culture among young Tanzanians. Creative arts and literature are integrated into school curricula, encouraging students to explore their artistic potential and appreciate the country's literary heritage.

Tanzania's cultural diversity and artistic expressions also contribute to its growing tourism industry. Visitors to the country have the opportunity to experience traditional music, dance performances, and visit art galleries that showcase the nation's creative spirit.

Infrastructure and Transportation: Connecting the Nation

In the vast and diverse landscape of Tanzania, a robust infrastructure and efficient transportation network are vital to connect its people, regions, and resources. As a developing nation, Tanzania has made significant strides in improving its infrastructure and transportation systems to facilitate economic growth, enhance connectivity, and improve the overall quality of life for its citizens.

Roads are the primary mode of transportation in Tanzania, linking cities, towns, and rural areas. The government has invested in road construction and rehabilitation projects to expand the road network and improve accessibility. Major highways, like the Tanzam Highway, connect the country to neighboring countries, facilitating regional trade and cooperation.

Transportation in Tanzania is not without its challenges, especially in remote and rural areas where road conditions can be difficult during rainy seasons. However, ongoing efforts are being made to address these issues and ensure that essential services and resources are accessible to all Tanzanians.

In recent years, there has been a significant focus on expanding and modernizing Tanzania's ports and harbors, recognizing the importance of maritime trade and transport. Dar es Salaam, Tanzania's largest city and commercial hub, boasts one of East Africa's busiest ports. The port handles a substantial volume of cargo, facilitating imports and exports for landlocked neighboring countries.

Moreover, the construction of the Bagamoyo Port, expected to be one of the largest deep-sea ports in Africa, is set to enhance Tanzania's trade capabilities and attract increased foreign investment to the region.

Inland waterways, such as Lake Victoria and Lake Tanganyika, also play a crucial role in transportation, particularly for the movement of goods and passengers between coastal and landlocked regions. Ferries and boats connect various islands and lakefront communities, providing essential links for commerce and travel.

The railway system in Tanzania dates back to colonial times, and the government has been working to revitalize and modernize it for more efficient and reliable transportation. The Central Line and TAZARA railway, which links Tanzania with Zambia, have been significant contributors to regional trade and movement of goods.

Air transportation is an essential aspect of Tanzania's connectivity, with several international airports providing gateways to the country. Julius Nyerere International Airport in Dar es Salaam and Kilimanjaro International Airport in Arusha are among the busiest airports in East Africa, serving as major hubs for tourism and trade.

Tanzania has also invested in regional and domestic air services to improve accessibility to remote areas and national parks. Smaller airports and airstrips have been developed to support tourism and ease travel for business and humanitarian purposes.

The growth of telecommunications infrastructure has been crucial in connecting Tanzanians across vast distances and enabling access to information and services. The country has seen significant expansion in mobile phone coverage, with widespread adoption of mobile technology for communication and financial transactions.

The government's commitment to infrastructure development is evident in the establishment of various agencies and authorities dedicated to overseeing and implementing projects. The Tanzania Roads Agency (TANROADS), the Tanzania Airports Authority (TAA), and the Tanzania Ports Authority (TPA) are among the institutions responsible for overseeing their respective sectors.

Challenges and Hopes for Tanzania's Future

As Tanzania stands at the crossroads of its future, the nation faces a myriad of challenges and opportunities that will shape its path in the coming years. While the country has made significant progress in various sectors, there are still significant hurdles to overcome to achieve sustainable development and ensure a better future for all Tanzanians.

One of the most pressing challenges facing Tanzania is poverty. Despite steady economic growth, a significant portion of the population continues to live in poverty, especially in rural areas. Access to basic services such as education, healthcare, and clean water remains limited for many citizens. Tackling poverty and reducing income inequality are critical priorities for the government and development organizations.

Education is another area that requires focused attention. While Tanzania has made strides in expanding access to primary education, challenges persist in ensuring quality education and reducing dropout rates. Investment in education infrastructure, teacher training, and curriculum development are essential to equipping Tanzanian youth with the skills they need to thrive in a rapidly changing world.

Healthcare is also a significant concern. Access to healthcare services, particularly in remote and underserved areas, remains a challenge. The government has been working to improve healthcare infrastructure, increase access to essential medicines, and enhance the training of healthcare professionals. Addressing maternal and child mortality rates and combating diseases like malaria and HIV/AIDS are key priorities in the nation's healthcare agenda.

Environmental conservation and sustainability are crucial in the face of climate change and growing population pressures. Deforestation, illegal wildlife trade, and improper waste management are environmental issues that require urgent attention. Tanzania's unique biodiversity and natural resources must be protected for the benefit of future generations.

Agriculture is a cornerstone of Tanzania's economy, employing a significant portion of the population. However, the sector faces challenges such as low productivity, reliance on rain-fed agriculture, and vulnerability to climate variability. Emphasizing agricultural innovation, modernizing farming practices, and investing in irrigation systems can help enhance food security and livelihoods for farmers.

Corruption and governance issues also pose obstacles to Tanzania's development. Eradicating corruption, ensuring transparency, and promoting good governance are vital for building trust in public institutions and attracting foreign investment.

In spite of these challenges, Tanzania's future holds great promise. The nation's rich natural resources, strategic location, and diverse cultural heritage provide a strong foundation for growth and prosperity. With proper investment and governance, sectors such as tourism, mining, and manufacturing have the potential to drive economic development and create job opportunities.

The government's commitment to the development agenda is evident in its various initiatives, including the Five-Year Development Plan and Vision 2025. These frameworks outline key strategies and priorities to propel Tanzania toward becoming a middle-income country by 2025.

Moreover, Tanzania's youthful population presents an opportunity for the nation's future. By investing in education, skills development, and entrepreneurship, the country can harness the potential of its youth to drive innovation, economic growth, and social progress.

Tanzania's regional integration efforts, such as participating in the East African Community (EAC) and the Southern African Development Community (SADC), open doors for increased trade, investment, and cooperation with neighboring countries.

Epilog

As we come to the end of this journey through Tanzania, we reflect on the vast wonders and complexities that make this East African nation so captivating. From its diverse landscapes, rich history, and vibrant culture to the challenges it faces and the hopes it holds for the future, Tanzania's story is one of resilience, growth, and transformation.

Tanzania's geographical diversity is awe-inspiring. From the iconic Mount Kilimanjaro, Africa's tallest peak, to the expansive Serengeti plains teeming with wildlife, and the stunning beaches of Zanzibar, every corner of this country holds a unique charm. The sheer beauty of its national parks, game reserves, and conservation areas is a testament to Tanzania's commitment to preserving its natural heritage.

As we delved into Tanzania's history, we discovered a tale of ancient civilizations, colonialism, and the hard-fought struggle for independence. The journey from Tanganyika to the United Republic reflects the spirit of unity that has shaped Tanzania's identity and strengthened its position in the global community.

The Tanzanian people are at the heart of the nation's story. Their cultural diversity, artistic expressions, and rich traditions showcase the richness of human experiences that thrive within Tanzania's borders. The Maasai, the Hadza, the Makonde, and the Swahili people are just a few examples of the vibrant tapestry of ethnic groups that coexist harmoniously, contributing to the nation's unique identity.

We explored Tanzania's cuisine, savoring the flavors of Swahili delicacies and the spice-infused paradise of Zanzibar. The country's culinary traditions are a reflection of its history and cultural influences, offering a delightful gastronomic experience to visitors and locals alike.

Tanzania's wildlife and natural resources are a source of pride and a responsibility to protect. Conservation efforts are critical to safeguarding the nation's biodiversity and preserving its invaluable ecosystems for future generations to enjoy.

While Tanzania has made significant progress in various sectors, it faces challenges that demand attention and action. Poverty, healthcare, education, and environmental sustainability are just a few of the areas where concerted efforts are required to secure a brighter future for all Tanzanians.

Yet, amidst these challenges lie the hopes and dreams of a nation. Tanzania's youth hold the key to unlocking its full potential, with their energy, creativity, and innovation poised to drive progress and prosperity.

As we bid farewell to Tanzania, we carry with us the memories of its breathtaking landscapes, its rich history, and the warmth and hospitality of its people. The journey through this fascinating nation has left an indelible mark, reminding us that, like Tanzania, we too have the power to overcome obstacles, embrace our diversity, and shape a future filled with hope and promise.

Tanzania's story is far from complete. The epilog we leave behind today is but a moment in time, a snapshot of a nation's journey. As Tanzania continues to evolve, its narrative will be written by the collective efforts and aspirations of its people. Let us remember the lessons learned, the beauty witnessed, and the challenges faced, and let us carry the spirit of Tanzania with us as we step forward into the unknowns of tomorrow.

And so, as we bid farewell to Tanzania, we do so with gratitude and awe, knowing that its story continues to unfold, offering the world a glimpse of the beauty, resilience, and potential that lies within this remarkable nation. May Tanzania's journey inspire us all to be stewards of our own destinies, to embrace diversity, and to nurture hope in the face of challenges, as we journey onward in the grand adventure of life.

Printed in Great Britain
by Amazon